D0060235

all in startup

LAUNCHING A
NEW IDEA
WHEN EVERYTHING
IS ON THE LINE

DIANA KANDER

WILEY

Published by John Wiley & Sons, Inc., Hoboken, New Jersey.
Published simultaneously in Canada.

For general information on our other products and services or for technical support, please contact
our Customer Care Department within the United States at (800) 762-2974, outside the United
States at (317) 572-3993 or fax (317) 572-4002.

Wiley publishes in a variety of print and electronic formats and by print-on-demand. Some material
included with standard print versions of this book may not be included in e-books or in print-on-demand.
If this book refers to media such as a CD or DVD that is not included in the version you purchased, you
may download this material at http://booksupport.wiley.com. For more information about Wiley products,
visit www.wiley.com.

Library of Congress Cataloging-in-Publication Data:
Kander, Diana.
      All in startup : launching a new idea when everything is on the line / Diana Kander.
         pages   cm
      ISBN 978-1-118-85766-3 (hardback)
         1. Entrepreneurship.   2. New business enterprises.   I. Title.
   HB615.K355   2014
   658.1'1—dc23
                                                        2013050101

ISBN 9781118857663 (Hardcover)
ISBN 9781118857762 (ePDF)
ISBN 9781118857670 (ePub)

Printed in the United States of America
10 9 8 7 6 5 4 3 2 1

To my best friend, Jason.
Thanks for picking me
for this crazy adventure every day.

Contents

Contents

Foreword

A lot has happened in the field of evidence-based entrepreneurship since I first published the *Four Steps to the Epiphany*. In it, I first proposed that startups weren't smaller versions of large companies, and that the traditional advice from investors—write a business plan and execute the plan—was wrong. The reality is that startups needed to *search* for a business model rather than *execute* a business plan.

Over the past decade, the concepts outlined in the book have grown into an international Lean Startup movement. The Lean Launchpad curriculum I teach at UC Berkeley, Stanford University, Columbia University, and UCSF is now being taught at hundreds of universities; over 250,000 students have taken the online version of the course, and the National Science Foundation is using the course to commercialize science as part of the NSF Innovation Corps program.

Even large companies facing continuous disruption have begun to understand the need for continuous innovation and the value of "getting out of the building" and testing their assumptions.

Despite all the progress we've made, there remain hundreds of thousands of would-be entrepreneurs who have yet to learn the concepts of evidence-based entrepreneurship. That's why this book is so important.

All In Startup makes lean concepts more accessible through a simple but powerful allegory to which readers will easily relate. Diana Kander helps readers understand the value of the lean approach by tying it to a memorable story.

While the other books in the evidence-based entrepreneurship field, such as *The Startup Owners Manual*, *The Lean Startup*, and *Business Model Generation*, explain the "how to" of this methodology, *All In Startup* explains the "why." Go behind the scenes of a startup and understand why the protagonist, Owen Chase, struggles to get his concept off the ground by following a traditional approach of starting a business. Then see the value that a lean methodology can bring to his enterprise as he learns a faster, more efficient way to launch companies.

This is a must read for anyone interested in launching a new product or business.

Steve Blank

A Letter from Thom Ruhe

Vice President of Entrepreneurship at the Kauffman Foundation

Stories are powerful teaching mechanisms because they engage more parts of our brain than traditional educational tools. When we read a textbook or attend a lecture, we use the language processing centers of our brain to translate words into meaning. But that's only a small portion of our brain. When we read a novel, our brains are firing on all cylinders. Our brains react to the story as if we were in the middle of the action, experiencing it ourselves, and our brains connect the material to our personal experiences.

This linkage of new knowledge to our own memory bank makes new information relatable and easier to retain. That's why I'm so excited about Diana Kander's use of a novel to teach modern entrepreneurship principles. It's just brilliant.

Entrepreneurial science has come a long way over the past 10 years. We've learned a lot about how to significantly reduce the number of startup failures and yet we haven't been able to properly communicate these lessons to the entrepreneurs that need them most. Until now.

All In Startup is the best explanation I've seen of the entrepreneurial process behind turning ideas into profitable businesses. Diana masterfully uses fiction to illustrate important concepts aspiring entrepreneurs must master while providing her readers with a taste of the emotional roller coaster endured by those launching something completely new.

This compelling story lets the reader see entrepreneurship through the eyes of a first-time entrepreneur. How many of us wish that we had a do-over where we could utilize the valuable lessons learned from our first adventure? *All In Startup* gives readers a safe view into what happens when you launch your venture in the wrong way. It vividly demonstrates the challenges entrepreneurs must overcome both in their venture and in their personal lives to find success, and it gives us a common language to understand and communicate startup challenges.

This book offers anyone thinking about launching an idea a road map for significantly reducing the risks along the way. Don't daydream about your idea any longer. Stop wasting valuable time and money planning for someday. Read this book and start acting on that great idea.

Introduction

This book is unlike any business book you have ever read. It's sexy and suspenseful and designed to "show you"—rather than "tell you"—how to turn an idea into a profitable business.

If you are thinking about starting a business or you're having trouble getting one off the ground, this book was written for you.

As an entrepreneur, an investor, and, most recently, a senior fellow for the Kauffman Foundation, I've spent thousands of hours working with entrepreneurs, only to find that the vast majority of people starting businesses are doing it wrong.

The statistics are scary. The overwhelming majority of startups fail. Even startups funded by outside investors, the cream of the startup crop, fail a staggering 75 percent of the time.

What causes all this failure? First, let me tell you what does not cause startups to fail. They don't fail because the founders lack passion or a willingness to work hard. They don't fail because the founders refuse to risk their life savings or because no one is willing to invest. Startups don't fail because the founders couldn't build the software or product necessary.

Truthfully, most failing entrepreneurs are passionate, hardworking dreamers who will risk everything, and try anything, to make their startup a success. They are great people. Great people pushing flawed concepts for which no one was ever going to become a paying customer. Startups fail because by the time the founders figure out that their idea isn't good enough, it's too late to make it better. They only realize that no one actually wanted their product or service after they've already run out of money.

Seriously, it's that simple.

But why does this happen?

How is it possible that with so many available resources and "How To" guides from successful entrepreneurs and investors, so few individuals are able to find success?

What can you do to significantly decrease a business's chances of failure?

This book answers those questions by telling you the story of Owen Chase. Owen's entrepreneurial journey is an amalgam of both my own experiences launching companies and those of the hundreds of entrepreneurs with whom I have worked in my role at the Kauffman Foundation.

I've learned that you can try to explain business concepts in a million different ways, but entrepreneurs really learn these lessons only when they witness or experience failure and success themselves. With that in mind, I wrote a novel instead of a textbook. Within these pages, you can live the startup experience and learn these lessons without actually having to go half-broke and full-crazy.

Owen's story communicates four simple but profound ideas that anyone can employ to significantly increase their likelihood of success.

You can choose to put down this book and ignore these ideas, but the statistics speak for themselves. Ignoring these four principles virtually guarantees that you'll join the hundreds of thousands of people every year who put their life and soul into a new venture only to watch it fail. And if you don't fail right away, your company will meet a fate that is arguably even worse: wandering the Earth for years as a zombie startup, never growing or making any money, just barely surviving.

Don't be a zombie. Open your mind to these four ideas:

IDEA 1: Startups are about finding customers, not building products.

No entrepreneur fails because he couldn't build his product. He fails because no one wanted to buy what he built.[1]

Here's how a startup typically works:

1. An entrepreneur gets an *idea* and his mind starts racing with all the possibilities of what it could turn into, the impact it could have on the world, and all the money it could generate.
2. Next, the entrepreneur *builds* his idea. He spends a lot of time and money trying to build the most comprehensive version of it, rarely showing it to anyone because he wants it to be perfect before potential customers see it. First impressions are everything!
3. Then, the entrepreneur *brands* his idea. He develops a catchy name and a logo. He purchases a domain and builds a web site. He creates marketing materials. This has to look professional, he tells himself.
4. Finally, he goes out looking for *customers* and, more often than not, strikes out big time, causing him to realize that something is wrong with his initial idea. He revisits the *idea* and starts brainstorming how to make it better. And then he repeats steps 1 through 4 all over again, spending a lot of time and money, without making any forward progress.

This is the **startup loop of despair**. It can last anywhere from a few months to a few years, all before the business generates any substantive revenues.

---

[1]Read that again. Because it's really important. You may have read studies that explained away business failure due to the founder's experience, lack of capital, poor location, management, and so on. But these are all just excuses for the real reason businesses fail: not enough customers.

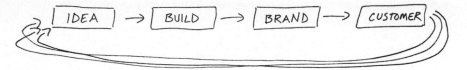

But successful entrepreneurs know that the startup loop of despair is completely avoidable. They know that once you come up with a great idea, the very next step should be to find potential customers and determine if your product is even worth building.

IDEA → CUSTOMER → BUILD → BRAND

Finding customers before building your product will guarantee that you will build a product people actually want by figuring out which features and benefits are the most valuable. Above all, this means your startup will actually generate revenue.

IDEA 2: People don't buy products or services; they buy solutions to their problems.

People don't go to the store looking for features and benefits. They don't walk down the aisles or surf the Web looking for the longest-lasting this or the least expensive that. They have problems that need solving. They shop because they can't get a stain out of their carpet, they can't reach their kids when they are out at night, or they are worried about having enough money for retirement. People look for things that can solve these problems, and they will pay money for them. These people are called *customers*.

The trouble with customers is that they are totally irrational and unpredictable. You can't assume that because you've diagnosed a problem, customers will agree with your assessment. Or, if they do consider it a problem, you can't assume that it's the kind of problem they'd pay money to solve.

For every Instagram or Pet Rock, there are hundreds of thousands of failures that never made a dime. For every Facebook or Snuggie, there are hundreds of thousands of zombie startups lurching around, mostly dead, clumsily bumping into one another at networking events.

The only way to find out if your customers have a problem worth solving and whether your idea solves that problem is to directly interact with them.

IDEA 3: Entrepreneurs are detectives, not fortunetellers.

Developing a business model that makes money is not a creative writing exercise. You can't just put your best guesses down on paper, wait for a bank or investor to believe your story, and then start executing on your plan. Unfortunately, no matter how smart you are, you can't predict the future.

What separates real entrepreneurs from daydreamers and wannapreneurs is the search for facts. Successful business owners understand that their initial ideas are filled with a number of assumptions, many of which, if guessed incorrectly, could change the entire trajectory of their business. The only way to determine whether your guesses are right is to test them in the real world.

Think that you can sell your product online rather than with a sales force? Test it. Think that you'll be able to find a huge partner that will distribute your idea for you? Test it. Think you can charge $49.99? Test it!

Don't waste time debating with investors, partners, or employees whether your guesses are right or wrong. Instead, spend the least amount of time and money gathering evidence that can prove or disprove your assumptions.

IDEA 4: Successful entrepreneurs are luck makers, not risk takers.

Most people assume that successful entrepreneurs are a lot like professional poker players—gamblers who take huge risks with their capital. The analogy is a good one because successful entrepreneurs and professional poker players do have a lot in common, but it's not what you'd expect. In reality, neither views himself as a gambler or a risk taker.

Instead, they have learned how to minimize risk and generate luck. They do this by making a series of small, calculated bets to test their assumptions and find new opportunities. Each small bet is something they can afford to lose because it's a small investment of time or money. Eventually, these strategic bets yield opportunities that both professional poker players and successful entrepreneurs will use all of their resources to exploit.

To the outside world it looks like they just get lucky a lot, but to the trained observer, they only go all in when they know they have the best chance of winning.

■　■　■

There are plenty of books written for those that want to chase the entrepreneurial dream. This is a guide for those that want to achieve it.

There is no secret DNA sequence or genetic lottery ticket necessary to find success at the end of the entrepreneurial path. No academic pedigree or corporate background can prevent the zombification of your startup. Learning and applying the lessons in this book will be the difference between playing entrepreneur and creating a real company.

By the time you finish this story, you'll be well on your way to finding customers and generating revenue—the only important measures of entrepreneurial success.

Chapter 1

First Appearances Can Be Deceiving

She was at the bar. Owen immediately knew it was her. He hadn't gotten the greatest look at her face on the treadmill at the gym, but he could tell from the hair and the shirt. Natural blonde and she was wearing another Sparksys shirt. Was she a sales rep? Owen wasn't as familiar with the company as he should have been. Having your own business really puts a damper on learning about other companies, especially ones where nobody is exactly sure what they do.

He knew Sparksys made an important part of microprocessors for smartphones and that somehow they'd managed to make that sexy. It wasn't deliberate advertising on their part, but they were known and featured in many magazines for the ridiculous perks their employees received. Owen wasn't sure, but he had read something about their offering something called the 7 C's, where every year for seven years they'd pay for a week or two-week or something visit to a different continent. That's insane. How much does that cost? Wait—that's just the kind of company that'd buy bicycles for its employees.

"Hey."

Owen looked down. The woman had approached him. She was definitely a sales rep. Women don't approach you in Vegas unless they're offering up some sort of service. Maybe it was callous, but the first thought that flashed through Owen's mind was: couldn't they pick a sales rep with bigger boobs? Oh well—he'd listen to her pitch, pretend to sound interested, and then possibly pick up the name of somebody he could contact about ordering bicycles. Maybe this was a win-win. Or a win for him at least. Not like she had a chance of selling him anything—ReBicycle didn't need smartphones for its employees. It barely needed employees.

"Hey, I'm Owen. What is Sparksys doing at the World Series of Poker?" A good lead-in question, Owen thought.

"How do you know I work for Sparksys?"

Shit. That quickly backfired. Owen didn't want to say he saw at her at the gym. That might come off creepy. At the same time, if she's in sales, she probably won't care. She wants people to look at her.

"The gym. You were wearing a Sparksys shirt there, too."

"Oh, was I?"

"Yeah. I mean I think it was you. Unless you have a doppel-ganger hanging around this hotel."

"You were at the gym?"

"Getting a little cardio in." Owen patted his stomach, "I'm play-ing in the World Series tomorrow and didn't want to overdo it, but at the same time, you can feel the stress in this place. Got to burn it off somehow."

"I agree. But it seems like most people here fall into the 'eat your stress' category." She gave him a big smile.

Owen responded with a nervous chuckle. It was a decent line. She was game. Laid-back approach for a salesperson, too. Owen liked and disliked that. He had dealt with enough people coming into ReBicycle trying to sell him dumb things he didn't need that he was constantly on guard. He knew she was going to ask him if he was aware of Sparksys's latest offerings and that she currently had one of their microprocessors in her contact lenses because they were so small or something like that.

She nodded toward the insignia on his polo shirt. "So what's ReBicycle?"

She was going for the sale. Owen could tell.

"ReBicycle? It's my company."

Owen had thought of plenty of good ideas for companies. His MBA and his Deloitte consulting job had put opportunities in front of him on a regular basis. He'd frequently think of startup ideas that might be worth something, but the more he slept on the ideas, the more doubt he developed about them. He'd never had that doubt with ReBicycle. It was solid. He could see it perfectly. He could hardly think about anything else. He knew people would love the value he was creating. He could provide for his family on his own terms. He could provide for a lot of families.

"I figured as much. So what is it? Should I have heard of it?" A nice unhurried question. She was good.

"Well, do you ride road bikes? Or do CAT races? We advertise all over the place. We're an online-based company that takes slightly used bike parts and we build custom-made bikes and then we sell them for a fraction of the cost of what the big bike companies do. It's all about delivering like a really amazing product. And at an affordable price point, which is a big problem in the cycling world."

She was quiet. Probably gearing up for the big pitch.

"Great, so how is it going?"

Ha! How's it going? Well, should he tell her that he's unable to make the payments on either his first or second mortgage? Maxed out on two credit cards? On the brink of laying off six people who put their faith in him, who put the well-being of their families in his hands?

Dammit! The bikes are ridiculously good and ridiculously cheap. How is it not growing? Shit, how is it not surviving? The bikes are literally half the price of the ones people can buy in a store. Half the price! We're talking 500 to 600 bucks. That's not chump change— that's a cruise.

His initial plan was flawless. Identify a problem. Check. Bicycles are expensive and good bicycles are really freaking expensive. Identify a solution. Check. Build bikes by hand from slightly used parts that are available and cheap. Identify a market. Check. People who are cost-conscious but know quality. Identify a way to reach those people. Check. Advertise on all the largest cycling forums, send free samples to the big magazines, set up booths at large trade shows. Generate word of mouth.

Check, check, check, check. ReBicycle had done all of those things. And yet ReBicycle had also sold only eight bikes in the past week. Eight bikes was what Owen had envisioned moving on a slow Monday morning. Not an entire day. Not an entire week. What the hell was going on? Sometimes when reading cycling forums where people bragged about their new bikes, he'd day-dream about ringing the doorbell of that person's house and then physically shaking them and showing them just how much money they'd wasted. He'd written some nasty comments on those forums recently. Someone had called him a troll. He didn't tell Lisa, his wife, about that. He didn't tell her much anymore.

Their strained communication over the past few days was nothing new, and Owen knew he was responsible. Whenever he looked at Lisa now, he no longer saw the twinkle in her eye that used to always make him smile. He only saw the reflection of a man who was putting his family in financial peril to chase a dream. He just couldn't overcome the enormous sense of guilt. He wondered whether their marriage would be able to survive all of this.

"Uh, how's it going? Really well. We've been fortunate enough to get some really incredible publicity, and traffic to our site is increasing virtually every month." Owen gestured an increasing growth curve with his arm.

"You must be pretty successful. I mean the market must be pretty big if you're coming out for the World Series of Poker. Is it international or just domestic?"

What a fraud. Owen couldn't afford a ticket to the World Series of Poker. He could barely afford the drinks at this bar. He was only here because last week, his best friend, Pitchford, entered a last-chance $300 buy-in tournament at Island Resorts, the local Columbus casino, where you could see from one end to the other and no drinks were free. Owen hated the place. It was a 200-person tournament and the top three finishers got a place at the World Series of Poker instead of cash. Pitchford had told Owen he was entering it, which was nuts because Pitchford was in the middle of getting ready to leave on a consulting project in Japan for six months. Pitchford had also told Owen that if he won, he was going to give Owen his spot at the WSOP. He placed second and kept his promise.

Owen didn't want to go. He couldn't go. It wasn't right to go. He told Pitchford as much. Pitchford told him he was an idiot if he turned down the deal of a lifetime. A free trip to Las Vegas and a free entry into the World Series of Poker, usually a $10,000 fee. Pitchford told Owen that they could split the winnings. Whatever Owen won, he could keep half. It'd be like they were playing on the same team.

Lisa was also surprisingly supportive . . . cautiously supportive. She said she thought the trip would help Owen clear his head, maybe figure out the best thing to do with the business. Who knew? Owen could actually win some serious money. It was an opportunity they really couldn't afford to pass up.

"Well, right now, we're just domestic. And the market is there . . . but uh . . . we've had some difficulties tapping into . . . uh . . . well, we are still pretty new and we haven't made the dent on the market I was hoping for. But we're getting there. Like I said, the web site traffic is up 50 percent this month alone, and the press has been great. It's just a matter of time. And what do you do for Sparksys?" Best to just change topics.

"Not much of anything anymore. I'm here to play in the tournament."

"You?"

"Yeah. Me. What's the matter? Never met a girl who could play poker?"

"So are you like a pro and you're sponsored or something?"

A genuine laugh from her, though Owen didn't mean it to be funny.

"I'm not a pro. I'm not sponsored. I am sober, though. I'm going to grab a drink. You need one?"

"Sure. I'd love to pick your brain on how Sparksys chooses its vendors."

A look of disgust flashed across her face. Disgust equaled wrinkles. Maybe she was older than her early thirties. Thirty-seven tops. Owen prided himself on being able to tell demographics. Why was she disgusted that he asked about Sparksys and potentially doing business with them? Definitely not a saleswoman. The chest, age, and demeanor ruled that out. What was she?

"What's your name?"

"Sam."

Chapter 2

You're Not
Fooling Anyone

Sam had immediately recognized him for what he was. He was in shape, wearing a work polo with sleeves that were too tight. The company logo and lack of funky glasses ruled out advertising industry. The tip-top shape, khakis, and polo screamed some hip business. He was a small-business owner who had hit it big or at least big enough to come to the World Series of Poker. Sam hadn't even really wanted to talk to him, but across the bar she couldn't make out the logo on his shirt. So she had approached. As she approached, he kept staring. An introduction was going to happen. She wasn't shy about that.

ReBicycle? What was that? Since selling Sparksys, Sam had followed plenty of startups. She was sure she had never heard of ReBicycle. She would have recognized the terrible name immediately. Was it possible she was losing her grip on startup news?

Sam's interest in ReBicycle was piqued. She had a feeling it was used bicycles of some sort, but the ambiguous name left it unclear. She was willing to put up with his small talk to find out. Plus, he was ultra-fit, although a little thin.

Sam's theory was confirmed when he didn't offer to buy her a drink in the first sentence. If he was looking to do the horizontal mambo with her this evening, he would have tried to pump alcohol in her at the earliest possible opportunity. As it was, she was going to have to pump alcohol in herself. Jeez, wouldn't founders like this guy ever learn to have fun, too?

After getting drinks—Sam noticed the man got Jack Daniel's straight. She liked what little she knew about him. He said he spied an open high table. Whatever. She'd sit with him for 20 minutes. What was his name again?

"What was your name again? I'm sorry. I'm terrible with . . ."

"No, it's okay. Owen. Sam, right? Short for Samantha?"

One strike against him. Captain obvious. She had a half-a-dozen witty responses to that very question, but she quickly spied his wedding ring, strike two. The allure was beginning to wear off. Probably just another successful businessman.

As he started talking about his business, however, Sam noticed that something was definitely off. His replies hit almost every red flag out there. Every entrepreneur wants to tell you they are doing great. It's the facade they have to create for potential customers, their employees, their investors, pretty much everyone they meet. Sam knew it all too well because she spent so many years telling everyone she knew how well things were going when she was on the very cusp of losing it all. She wondered if she could crack him. Figure out what was really going on.

"Well, obviously, you've been very successful with your company or you wouldn't be here. Cheers to the profits." She lifted her glass.

He didn't cheer. He just stared at her for a moment as if he was scrolling through a Rolodex of possible responses.

"We've still got a long way to go."

Ha! . . . that didn't take very long. He's already starting to crack. This guy must be pretty new at convincing others of how well things are going.

"I've actually been thinking a lot about expanding our business to corporate clients, and I don't know much about Sparksys, but I do know that they are known for taking care of their employees. What better way to encourage fitness than giving them bicycles? Or offering them at a subsidized rate?"

Damn. This guy didn't seem interested in opening up, nor was he trying to get in her pants. He was just going for the hard sale quick. Time to burst his bubble.

"Well, that's great—Owen, right? But I don't work for Sparksys. I didn't really maintain any ties there after I left."

Visible disappointment.

"Oh . . . so let me ask you, if they treat their employees so great, why did you quit?"

"I didn't quit."

"Oh, they . . . let you go?"

Ughh. Sam rolled her eyes. This was always hard to explain without being totally honest.

"I sold it, okay? I'm the founder."

Visible surprise.

She hadn't been meaning to tell him she was the founder, but now she had and she knew he'd have a ton of questions. She wasn't going anywhere for a good hour. It didn't matter.

And that was the problem Sam was having with everything right now—not much mattered. For seven years Sparksys had been her life. She finally sold it two years ago after her marriage ended and was still suffering heavily from seller's remorse. She thought about the company a lot more than the marriage.

She had been at fault for the breakup. Not only did Sparksys eat up every hour of her life, but she had made out with the reporter from *Wired* who covered the company. A little more than made out actually. But whatever—cheating is cheating. It was a moment of weakness on her part. You make amends and move on—that was her motto. So why couldn't she move on from Sparksys?

Her business card now listed her as "Investor," but she was often one of many investors in a deal. She couldn't drive ideas the way she had with Sparksys. More worrisome, she didn't have the desire. She blamed that on the fact that she hadn't counted on people having so many terrible ideas when she decided to become an investor. (But then again, the guy who invented the Snuggie made a fortune, so who knows what counts for terrible anymore?)

At Sparksys, Sam had always considered herself a good boss. She was a big proponent of not just caring for people but caring *about* people. She stayed on really good terms with many of her ex-employees. When she started investing, she thought that she could act the same way. Friendly, cooperative, offering constructive criticism. She quickly learned that did not work with entrepreneurs. People are so tied up in their ideas, that they take any positive language as a green light for full-steam ahead. They just couldn't hear what she was really trying to tell them. In the first six months, she found herself nodding her head a lot, offering a lot of advice, but not committing any money.

By the seventh month, something clicked—or snapped, depending on your perspective. She remembered the first guy that got a dose of what she now called "the treatment"—he had invented some lawn thing. He was a weekend gardener and he was convinced that his invention was the second coming of the cotton gin. Within five minutes Sam knew it would fail.

She asked the guy how many customers he had. He said he needed capital to get started. She asked how many potential customers he had spoken with, and he replied that he wanted to wait until he could show them the finished product, but he was confident it would be successful because of his expertise in the industry. The product would "sell itself."

Sam let him have it. She explained that the invention wouldn't sell itself. That the product was not the business. He had no business model to speak of and no interactions with potential customers to let him know whether he was on the right track. He needed serious help. He didn't even argue back. Pansy.

An Allman Brothers' song came on at the bar. It was a nice reprieve from the Radiohead and other depressing music the bar had been playing. Why play depressing music the day before the WSOP? Most of these people were going to leave depressed anyway. Sam figured she would enjoy the song before Owen's questions started.

She still couldn't tell if he was the type that would cheat on his wife.

Chapter 3

You Can't Sell Anything by Doing All of the Talking

O wen couldn't sleep. His mind was racing. His conversation with Sam kept replaying over and over again in his mind. Try to focus on the wife. Try to focus on the wife. All right, try to focus on Pitchford and whatever poker advice he would offer if he were here. Try to focus on the World Series of Poker tomorrow. No use. It was still Sam.

People have a natural tendency to mentally replay conversations that they deem unique, like talking to a pretty girl who was not his wife or talking to an influential entrepreneur. Sam was both of those things. Owen's instant analysis of the conversation was that he had talked too much. Way, way too much. Did she yawn? He didn't think so. No, she seemed genuinely interested. But not all the way interested. Why would she be? ReBicycle wasn't her baby. She had no emotional attachment to it.

So then why did she listen to him for a solid hour? He still didn't know a damned thing about Sparksys. Were those stories of Hot Air Balloon Fridays true? They couldn't be—Sam didn't strike him that way. She seemed to understand him, though. Like, on every level.

She kept nodding her head when he talked about how passionate he was about ReBicycle. How once the idea took hold of him, he could hardly think of anything else. How his work at the consulting firm started to seem so unimportant. How he kept seeing signs of why this was such a great idea everywhere he went. She completely seemed to understand his desire to do things differently. To create his own thing that provided a much-needed product for consumers. A company that treated its employees like associates and created an atmosphere where people were excited to come to work, all focused on a single vision. He was getting all worked up.

Once he and Lisa had decided to take the leap, he became numb to anything at the consulting firm. None of it mattered. There was actually an overlap of several weeks where the site was live and he was still technically working at the firm, but he had mentally checked out months ago. He had worked on the business plan for over six months and knew everything there was to know about the bicycle market when the site went live in June. A little rushed but he had to catch as many of the warm months as he could.

The crew was Owen, several mechanics to actually assemble the bikes, a guy he hired off Craigslist named Gary to secure wholesale parts, the Web designer, two marketing interns, and Lisa doing the books. The original business plan called for more mechanics and only one marketing guy, but Owen figured he needed the PR push at the beginning, and then after things got rolling and the brand name recognition was there, he could shift one of the marketing positions to a different role.

ReBicycle's headquarters was in the industrial part of town. It was all vinyl siding and aluminum from the outside, but inside, it felt like a startup. Owen had brought in a ping-pong table. There was always decent music playing over the PA, and even a kegerator for celebrations, and there were plenty of things to celebrate in those early months.

Owen was focused on creating a great work environment. It was important to him that everyone felt invested in his vision and was able to create their own personal growth plan. He was going to not only create a successful company, but shape lives. He remembered the early months of coming into the office. He couldn't wait to experience all the sights and sounds waiting for him there. The impromptu beer pong games, the guerilla marketing campaigns, and how the whole office tried to outdo itself to celebrate someone's birthday.

But somehow the excitement and hard work was not translating into sales. Everyone was busy and seemed to be productive, but they weren't meeting any of Owen's business plan projections. Not even close.

The big redesign of ReBicycle had been in the spring. After several months of slow sales, Owen had asked for ideas from friends in a couple of different industries. He learned that his site wasn't user friendly enough and had poor search engine optimization. The redesign had gone really well. He had the numbers to prove it. A 200 percent increase in traffic the first month. Owen reiterated the words 200 percent. Sam didn't seem impressed. Didn't she know that was unheard of? Forget it, she doesn't know about cycling. She doesn't know the market. Why was he even sharing all of this with her?

Looking back, Owen knew this was the moment when he should have engaged Sam. It was clear as day. This was the moment to get her opinion. But he kept on talking. What a schmuck sometimes.

The reason he kept on talking and the reason he was probably losing his hair was that the increase in traffic hadn't led to an increase in sales. That was also unheard of—you get more eyeballs, you get more clicks, you get more sales. Owen had preached that time and time again at his consulting job.

Was this the point when Sam possibly yawned?

He decided not to tell her about the mounting personal debt. What was it up to now? $300,000? $400,000? He didn't tell her that he was days away from just shutting the entire company down. That he couldn't remember the last time he celebrated with the team because of the immense sense of guilt he felt for having failed to lead them. He didn't tell her that he probably would have shut it down months ago, but he just couldn't admit that he had failed. Failed at something everyone who knew him thought was a sure thing. And he couldn't even think about firing everyone. It made him sick to his stomach. It kept him awake one sleepless night after the next. It made him avoid eye contact with his employees at all interactions. What few interactions he allowed now.

But maybe meeting Sam wasn't just a coincidence. Maybe she presented an opportunity to turn it all around.

"So what are you telling me?" she asked.

Owen thought about it for a second. The Jack Daniel's was feeling good. Who cared about poker tomorrow? She had listened this much, so he might as well go for it. Only one right move here, as Pitchford would say.

"I know . . . well, let me say I don't know. I don't know what your noncompete agreement is with the guys who bought Sparksys, but I can't imagine it includes bicycles. This company is going to be huge. It's only a matter of time before copycats try to enter the market. I just know the potential is there. We're circling this market like a lion." Good analogy. "We're ready to strike now. I know. And look, you're obviously a successful entrepreneur. If you'd be willing to invest or introduce me to people who would listen to my business plan and invest, I'd be . . . well, we could talk about a percentage stake of ReBicycle."

She rubbed her eyes. She was thinking it over! She knew it was a good idea! She was . . . she was . . . wait . . . What was Sam doing?

Reaching into her purse for something. Oh, her wallet. She put money on the table.

"Owen, you're . . . well, the short answer is no. Just no. Have a good night. See you at the tournament. Thanks for the drinks."

And with that, Sam had left. She'd spoken how many words? Why did she thank him for the drinks when she had paid? Why did she seem to agree with him the whole time and then just bolt?

Then it had dawned on him—shit, I didn't even get her card.

Chapter 4

It's How Well You Lose, Not How Well You Win, That Determines Whether You Get to Keep Playing

O wen woke up with a slight hangover. Truth be told, he wasn't a Jack Daniel's drinker, and he remembered now how dumb it was to order a drink you don't like just to impress a pretty girl. It was 8:30 A.M. With all the tossing and turning he did, that meant he'd slept for maybe four hours. That's not how he had planned to start the first day of the tournament. Today was going to be rough.

He hadn't even cracked open the David Sklansky poker book he'd brought along as a refresher on what Pitchford called "the advanced, kung-fu, special forces shit."

It wasn't really the first day of the tournament. Due to the large number of registrations for this year's WSOP and the limited number of poker tables they could fit into the grand tournament room, the first round had to be divided over three days, with roughly 2,400 players per day being whittled down to 900. Technically, this was the second day of the tournament. Owen had watched some of the play the day before. To say he was not impressed was an understatement. It might be the world's most prestigious poker tournament, but at the moment it was total pandemonium. Players going all-in on 4-5 off-suit, others literally betting every single hand or doubling the pot preflop only to check to the river and fold. Amateur hour. Maybe his day would be different.

"Ladies and gentlemen, welcome to the World Series of Poker. On the table in front of you, you should have exactly $30,000 in chips. At this time, please recount your chips to ensure that you have exactly . . ."

The announcer was reciting the opening of the tournament with all the excitement of a corpse. It would have been a letdown if Owen's blood hadn't been pumping so hard. He didn't think it would be. After all, he wasn't half the poker player or fan that Pitchford was. It wasn't his money. He didn't even want to be here. And though the announcer was obviously a wet sock, there was still a current in the air. All the players could feel it. Everybody seemed nervous. This was truly the World Series.

As for the table makeup, it was so-so. All men—not that rare an occurrence, though younger than he would have thought. Owen was priding himself on being a relatively fresh face, but two kids at this table would still get carded for cigarettes. In addition to the tots was an older man from Ghana who kept laughing and trying to banter with the table. He had one line—"oh no you didn't!"—which he'd try to say in an American accent. He was very good at cracking himself up. Pretty good guy. Probably came from nothing and was an amazing success story. Or maybe he was a dictator or something. Enough! Focus on the cards.[1]

Owen was definitely nervous. He hadn't paid the $10,000 entry fee. He knew no one expected him to win—or even make it past the first couple of hours—but he was nervous all the same. He looked around the room to see if he could identify any players he'd seen on television or anyone he knew. He'd watched the WSOP on TV and the room had seemed so big. And it was. But with so many people crammed around tables and another mass watching behind cordons, the room felt positively tiny. Plus, it smelled overwhelmingly of cologne. Was that Brut? In a way, it reminded Owen of senior prom—a lot of people who don't know what they're doing in a small space with unrealistic expectations. He hadn't scored at prom. Hopefully, that wasn't an omen.

Because of his nervousness and the crappiness of his pocket cards, Owen folded a lot for the first four hours. When he did play, it was always with really strong face cards or pairs on his initial pocket cards, and he was aggressive. No bluffing yet. But mostly he folded. Blinds were so low that even with Owen having to play every ninth hand, if he folded or just called to get to the flop, he could always fold with barely any loss. Despite what he'd seen on

---

[1] For those who have limited experience with Texas Hold 'Em, the ground rules are simple enough: You get two cards dealt to you and you alone face down. You don't show anyone these "pocket cards"—ever—not even your mom. Based on the strength of these two cards, you make a bet or, if they aren't strong enough to play, you say screw it and fold.

To make sure there is something at stake in every hand, two players are chosen in a rotating clockwise fashion to bet in every hand; one guy is forced to bet a lot (big blind), and one guy is forced to bet half of the big blind (the little blind). From then on, the game is based on three, and only three, choices: (1) folding; (2) calling, which is matching the amount already bet; and (3) raising. The no-limit in No-Limit Hold 'Em refers to the amount a player can raise. Anyone and everyone can literally bet all of their chips on one hand, one card even. If you win, you continue on. If you lose . . . well you join the other 7,199 people who will also eventually lose. And once you lose, that's it—you're out. Good job and see you next year. Sounds simple enough, right? Yeah, add a $10,000 buy-in fee, television cameras, and pros with MIT degrees who play 50-plus hours a week, and you can see why people get nervous. Nervousness does not translate to good play.

the previous day of play, Owen had assumed this was most people's strategy. He'd assumed incorrectly.

Poker's version of Darwin's Law was taking place on an almost continual basis. People were going all-in at extraordinary rates. Twice in the first four hours he saw two players he'd pegged as having a similar playing style as his get sucked into all-in hands. All it took was a belief that you had the best hand after the flop (the first three community cards). And maybe you did, but there was still the fourth card (the turn) and fifth card (the river). Anything could happen with those cards. Tournaments have been won on the river card. Many players have been eliminated because their opponent hit a river card he shouldn't have. Divorces definitely have happened because of this—Owen was pretty sure he was hearing one about 100 feet away.

Because so many players were betting and betting big, the cast of characters Owen was playing against kept changing. The cigarette-carded boys were soon replaced by baggy sweatshirt guy and Asian man of ambiguous origin. They, too, were replaced by Larry the house painter (chill dude, made no secret that he paid for his entry by selling marijuana plants on the side—love to see ESPN put that banner up when Larry makes the finals) and the annoying guy from "Detroit Proper" who made everyone at the table promise to get a drink with him after the tournament. He was the one who knocked out the Ghana missionary/dictator. Oh no he didn't!

Really, though, it reminded Owen of working at a gas station in college. Owen had mainly worked the overnight shifts for three long years, partially because they fit around his class schedule and partially because the owner refused to fire his shitty brother, who always worked the prime shifts. Owen had been robbed at gunpoint twice. He'd seen a guy OD in the bathroom. He had learned to tell the difference in the blink of an eye between the guy coming in at 3 A.M. who was a drug dealer looking to cause trouble and the one who was just a lost soul. Drug dealers always had clean shoes. Owen could quickly size up his opponents. But on that first day, there were so many people coming and going that, besides one or two characters, everybody just blended together. After all, how many heavyset, rich white dudes in polo shirts and sunglasses can you remember? Instead, Owen remembered hands.

The most memorable by far that first day came around hour seven. If playing poker is a marathon, hour seven is the point at which your body has consumed its natural energy reserves. Owen's chip stack had dwindled slightly. He'd won several times, but nothing big, and the blinds were eating away at his stack throughout the day.

Besides a couple queen-king off-suits, his highest face pair had been a pair of jacks. He was in the big blind and honestly a little bit bored when he hit pocket kings, the second strongest starting hand in poker. He entered strong and tripled the big blind. Having rotating partners at a table was a blessing in that a lot of the new people at Owen's table didn't know his conservative style and three fools called.

All right, Owen thought, even if everyone folded right after the flop, he'd still get back to even money for the day. The flop was a thing of beauty. Two low cards and a king. Almost too strong. Owen didn't want to bet now and risk scaring off the three fools. After each fool checked, Owen made a small bet to test the waters. Was it too small? Would they see through it? The first player folded. Shit— they're not all fools. But no, the other two called. All right, we've got ourselves a game.

The turn card was a 9. Just high enough to give Owen hope one of the other two guys might bet. Sure enough, the kid in the Michigan jersey raised. The other player folded, and it was to Owen. Owen thought about raising, decided against it, and was about to say "I call" when Michigan jersey guy twitched just a little. Almost subconsciously, something about that subtle twitch made Owen pause. For the first time all day, his instincts were talking to him. "I raise," said Owen, counting out a short little stack and calmly placing it next to his previous bets. Immediately, Michigan jersey guy pushed all of his chips toward the middle, "all-in."

Michigan jersey guy had two nines in the pocket. Once he saw Owen's hand, he knew. He was gone from the table before the river card came down—it wasn't a nine—and with that, Owen started shoveling his winnings toward his corner of the table. It was a surreal, almost out-of-body experience. Here he was in the World Series of Poker, collecting a huge pot. He heard a smattering of applause and a lone "whoo." He wasn't sure if it was intended for him.

Oh well, he'd take it no matter who it was meant for—he was alive, baby!

Chapter 5

The Real Pros Don't Play Every Hand

S am hadn't planned to watch the second day of the tournament. She wanted to get a massage—it was always a good way to relax and kill a couple of hours, and she needed a new laptop or at least she needed to start considering a new laptop—but really those were just time wasters. She was getting antsy. She'd been in Vegas for a few days now, and the Main Event of the World Series had started the day before, but she wouldn't play her first day of poker until tomorrow.

She was determined to at least beat her lousy performance in last year's tournament. She had at one point been in the top 100 in terms of chips, only to get a run of bad cards and be eliminated on the second-to-last hand of the first day. This time she would deliberately ease off the pedal. Not get cocky. Not let her emotions get the best of her.

But no matter how ready she was to play, today she was still a bystander. Yesterday had been unproductive. She'd gotten a massage, hung out in downtown Vegas with a friend, and even shopped for clothes—something she despised. She didn't want her friend to feel like he had to babysit her the entire time. At least that was the justi- fication she gave herself for staying at the hotel bar last night instead of going out with her friends. She still couldn't figure out how she got roped into an hour-long conversation with used bike guy.

She smiled. She secretly liked Owen. His idea was god-awful, but his passion was obvious in the way he talked about it. She had once had that passion. That belief in a greater purpose. She missed the moments that she had epiphanies. She missed the sales calls. She missed those first employees. Damn, she missed it all. Owen was headstrong, but was he moldable, too? Oh well, who cares? Not like she was going to reach out to him. If he wanted to find her, he could.

More than any other factor, it was Phil Helmuth, the poker pro known for his bluster at the table, who brought Sam to the tourna- ment floor today. Sam thought he was a jerk. She had bumped into him once in Atlantic City and he confirmed her impression. Word on the street was that he was playing on the second day. She decided she would look for him from the peanut gallery. Also, it didn't hurt that they allowed alcohol in the peanut gallery.

By the time Sam actually reached the tournament floor and found Phil at a table with two other big-name pros, there was a crowd three-deep trying to watch the action—or lack of it. Forget it; there had to be other people to watch today. If there was one thing Sam wasn't, it was a herd follower.

Sam found herself interested in a player a few tables from the Helmuth action. She mentally referred to him as Neon Green. Not his real name, of course. Like many players, he wore sunglasses, but his were neon green. That in and of itself wasn't too spectacular. What was amazing was his style of play. Not how good it was—but the opposite. Sam was slack-jawed as she saw Neon Green win a series of hands in which the only two times he was actually forced to show his cards at the end of the hand revealed a 2-8 off-suit and a 9-10 off-suit. Yet people genuinely feared him—like he had a special power.

She was mesmerized by Neon Green. She enjoyed watching him play and, even better, watching others react to his outlandish style. It was clear from his body language, his demeanor, his entire everything that he was in over his head. Yet he kept winning! God bless this tournament. Sam knew this couldn't last much longer. Like an eager entrepreneur, Neon Green came to the tournament today too excited to play. He likely thought this tournament was an exciting thrill ride where he needed to make the most out of every second. The real pros were calm, objective, and waiting for the right moment to strike, not just excited to play in every hand.

By the end of the day, Neon Green had lost most of his money. His wild play and betting style had stopped producing big wins. All of a sudden he seemed scared. Other players had caught onto his game and his erratic behavior was no longer yielding any results. Sam had lost track of time. She must have been following Neon for two hours. She was pretty buzzed. Neon had gotten up to go the restroom and didn't look to be returning. She looked around.

Two tables over from Neon she spied an old friend. No wait. Not an old friend. But someone who looked familiar just the same. It was Owen. He was still in. Good for him. Sam thought about saying hello, but it was clear that he was busy. He had a sizable bet on the table and he looked sweaty. Almost clammy. Definitely not the guy in the bar last night. No wonder ReBicycle was failing if he acted this nervous in business presentations. Well, besides a whole list of other issues with ReBicycle. She actually had some thoughts about it when she woke up. Should she write them down and send them to him? She got his business card, right?

Somewhere within that train of thought, she sized up Owen's situation at the table. He was pretty low on chips and was going head-to-head with a kid in a baggy hooded sweatshirt. Within about two minutes of her watching, the sweatshirt kid called all-in. She held her breath as the pocket cards were revealed.

As soon as Owen laid down his kings, he straightened up, took a deep breath, and grinned. It was like that nervousness had been an act. Was it an act? Damn, he had an athletic jawline. The two guys on either side of her lazily clapped. She found herself clapping as well. Then she heard herself yell, "whooo!" Where had that come from? She hadn't meant to. Guess it felt pretty good watching somebody you sort of know win a clutch hand. Would Owen be at the bar tonight?

Chapter 6

Vanity Metrics Can Hide the Real Numbers That Matter to Your Business

S o this is what being high feels like. Not that Owen had never felt like this, but in the past year or so it had just been one difficult day to one setback to bad news to . . . well, he wasn't going to worry about that. The endorphins were running, and it felt good to have his first poker high. For the first time, Owen could see why Pitchford was as addicted as he was to poker—it's not the winnings, it's the thrill of winning.

He'd made it through the first day of the tournament. That was better than he'd been willing to publicly speculate, though in reality he knew he didn't really do much—just played ultra-conservative and got lucky. Looking ahead, he had a pretty weak stack and was still a long way from the money. He'd have to change his style over the next day or so if he actually wanted to stay in. The blinds were going to start dramatically increasing soon. Whatever—he could think about that tomorrow. Due to the huge number of players, tomorrow was another off day. Maybe he'd read Sklansky's book or maybe, well, maybe he'd go for a bike ride. But what about now?

"Hi, Owen."

"Heeeyyyyyyy baby . . . how ya doing?"

Owen drew out his words. He was sprawled out on the hotel bed. He had decided to call Lisa. Suddenly, though, when he hit the bed and pressed her name on his phone, all of the energy he was feeling zapped away. He was tired. Content but tired. It was like being on pain meds.

"Well, you know. Work sucks. I got into it again with Joan. And I had to call CPS on Michael . . . again. But those jerks still refuse . . ."

Lisa was off and running. She still worked at the school but now as an administrator, and she didn't make any secret of hating it. She wanted to quit. Owen told her to quit. He told her she could help with ReBicycle full time. But the reality of the past year meant they both knew that was a fantasy. The end result was that Owen listened to Lisa's Variation-on-Same-Rant-as-Always. He'd heard the tune about a thousand times and still didn't care. Lisa never took his advice so he had long ago stopped giving it.

"Honey, that sounds terrible. Joan is . . . well, you know. I can't believe they keep her. Anyway, you wanna hear some good news? I made it today. Through day one. I'm still in the tournament."

"Really? That's great. How much have you won?"

"Well, I've got about $70,000 in chips right now, which is okay. Not the strongest but pretty good."

"Are you kidding? That's amazing! Seventy thousand dollars?!"

"Well, it's not $70,000 in cash. If I lose tomorrow, then I still get nothing. I've got to make it to the top 650 players or so."

Owen tried his best to gently explain that it was still Monopoly money at this point. He talked about his strategy, how the tiers of payouts worked so that if he did make it to the top 650, then he'd at least get $20,000. Once Lisa understood that it was not real, she seemed about as interested as he was in her rants. But he still talked. That was part of the deal of being married. You had to listen, but then you got to talk.

"Oh, you want to hear more great news?"

"Sure." Owen had more poker stories to share, but he could take a quick break for her change of subject.

"You know Stephanie, one of the fourth grade teachers, right?"

"Yeah." He had no idea which one she was.

"She's pregnant again! Isn't that great? I can't believe it."

This had nothing to do with Stephanie. Owen knew what it was. Just another excuse to talk about having kids. But there was nothing Owen could say other than, "Hey. That's great."

He had learned long ago that sarcasm about this topic only made Lisa angry. Trying to explain why he didn't feel ready to have kids brought her to the same ferocious emotional state. This was a trap, and all he could do was keep his head down and wait for it to pass.

"I mean, she's only 25 and already having her third kid. That's amazing. I don't even know if we can have that many by the time we start trying. That's just a lot of kids to try to cram into a really small window."

Well, that didn't take long, Owen thought. "Listen, honey, I want to keep talking, but I'm just so exhausted from today. Just concentrating for 12-plus hours really takes it out of you, you know?"

She got the hint. She quickly changed topics to something about the house.

Owen knew Lisa didn't give a rip about poker. He secretly thought she didn't give a rip about cycling. The first year of dating she had been so interested in it, but, looking back, it was always to be around him. Owen had promised to try some of Lisa's hobbies, but she didn't seem to have many. She liked going shopping but that was a release, not a hobby. And she loved dogs. But again, that's not a hobby, that's a pet. They had tried date night over the past year off and on. When it was his turn to pick, Owen would try to find something new that she might latch on to—rock climbing, driving range, skeet shooting, even Bikram yoga. Something to get her active again. Lisa always chose the same thing on her turns—dinner and a movie. It seemed like she was already set to be a stay-at-home mom. The only thing missing was a baby.

Owen found himself wandering . . . daydreaming and just grunting approvals or "uh-huhs" to Lisa. He couldn't remember the last time they had sex. That was pathetic. Was it two or three weeks ago?

". . . so do you want me to e-mail you the sales results from this weekend?"

Lisa was talking business. Owen was back in.

"How do we look?"

"I don't want to e-mail them. They're not good."

"How not good?"

"Two bikes not good."

"All weekend?"

"Including Friday. I know a lot of people are taking vacations this week. And gas went up again. Don't think that helped . . ."

"So we only sold two bikes over a three-day period?"

"Tell me about it, Owen. What do you want me to do?"

"I don't know . . . I don't . . . do you have the site stats there as well?"

"Uhh . . . hold on . . . so here we are. I'm sure you've checked them online but well . . . whoa. We actually had a 15 percent trailing week bump."

"I haven't checked them since I've been here. But 15 percent?"

"Yeah, 15.4 percent to be exact. 800-plus first-time viewers. A couple hundred repeat visitors. Maybe everybody is holding off?"

Owen didn't know what to think. The online ads must be working that's for sure. But getting that many new visitors and so few sales was like being told you're handsome while being kneed in the groin—it was still unpleasant.

"Hey, thanks. I'll take a look at those stats. You got anything else?"

"No . . . I'm going out with Margaret tomorrow night for a girl's night . . ."

Lisa talked some more. Owen was still stunned by the stats. It was amazing how quickly his high was fading. It seemed like a week ago he was playing poker. That was less than an hour ago.

". . . Well, honey. Have fun with In-Charge Marge—not too much fun."

"Same to you, mister."

"On my best behavior."

"Good. Make sure you keep it that way."

Chapter 7

You Won't Find a Mentor if You Don't Ask

U gh . . . running two days in a row sucked. Sam had practiced six days a week in college on the cross-country team. Now the pain from her left knee was resonating throughout her body. And she wasn't even through the first mile yet. Breathe. Lower the incline to zero. Take some pressure off the knee. Make sure to land on the front of your feet. Focus on form.

Sam knew she couldn't afford to get injured. Her metabolism wasn't what it once was, yet she still liked to drink. Sometimes, she liked to drink a lot. And drinking had so many calories. The world was mean like that. Running is what kept her thin. She still looked good naked—a point of great pride.

Besides, running was the sensible thing to do. She had to play in the morning. She needed to stay focused. She had never made it past the second day. Her personal best was her first time in the tournament when she was knocked out in the afternoon of the second day. This would be her year. Just stay focused, Sam.

She made it three miles. Right at 25 minutes. Not too fast and not slow. A couple more minutes to stretch, a little core work. Take a few peeks in the mirror. Still got it. She'd go to her room, turn off her cell phone, take another awesome Vegas hotel shower and be refreshed for tomorrow.

She was refilling her water bottle when she spotted Owen. Did he spot her as well? If not, she could hide in the corner. Actually, it wasn't that awkward to talk to him. She was just still a little embarrassed by her whoop. He was pretty interesting. Also . . . wow, those were some legs. They were oaks. Sam was that rare breed—a leg girl—and Owen had 'em.

This time he approached her.

"Hey."

"Well, there he is. The champion."

"Ha . . . how did you know?"

"Did you not hear me? I saw you win that all-in with the pocket kings."

"You saw me?"

"Saw you? I was your biggest cheerleader. Did you seriously not hear me?"

"Maybe . . . I just assumed . . . so were you knocked out already?"

"No. I didn't play today. I play my first day tomorrow."

"Oh . . . really? You saw me? Huh? Not too bad, right? I'm happy."

"Good. Glad you're happy."

Pregnant pause.

"Well, I've got play in the morning . . ."

"Hey, Sam. Wait. I'm not . . . well, I'm happy but I'm not happy. I want to talk to you."

"We're talking."

"You know what I mean. It's about business. It's about ReBicycle. Things may not be as great as I made them seem yesterday. And today, my wife told me some news. I'm not exactly sure what it means. Look, this isn't easy for me. Okay. I . . . ."

"What are you asking, Owen?"

"I want to run some things by you. You obviously know about starting a business if you started Sparksys."

"Okay. But I've got to play in the morning. Why don't you come up with a list of questions, e-mail them to me, and then I'll answer them."

"Look, it won't take long. I just want to get your take."

Sam looked around. The clock said 9 P.M. Even if she took the world's longest shower and ate, that'd take her only up to 10 P.M. She didn't naturally get tired until 11 or so.

"Okay, here's the deal, Owen. You want to talk. We'll talk. Two things. First, I'm all sweaty and I need a shower. Once I'm up in the room, I'm not going to feel much like getting all dressed up to go talk somewhere. I'm not leaving my room tonight. I've got to play in the morning. So if you want to talk, you have to come to my room. I'm going to have on sweatpants, probably be watching some television show, and if I feel like it, I'll give you some advice."

"I'll take it."

He seemed to accept that pretty eagerly. Did he have something else in mind besides shop talk? She didn't think so, but hey, those legs were something to behold in person. And he didn't shave them, which most cyclists do. She dated a cyclist in college and couldn't stand that. Back to the point. What was the point?

"Oh, and secondly, you've got to listen. I listened to you talk about ReBicycle for like what—six hours the other night? I actually gave it some thought. Believe it or not, I've been in your shoes. So once you enter that room, you agree to listen. Comprende?"

It was business Sam talking—the Sam that was full of testosterone and scared men. She'd learned to speak like that from other investors, and now it came naturally. It wasn't bravado for the sake of bravado—she needed Owen to know that she was serious. Scared Straight, the Entrepreneur Edition.

"Comprende."

"My room is 1108. If you knock after 10 P.M., I won't answer."

"Got it."

"Oh, and don't eat. I don't want to eat alone."

Chapter 8

Put Your Customers and Their Needs before Your Vision for a Solution

O wen was not impressed. Sam's room was no different than his own, even though it was several floors higher. She was sitting on the couch in a T-shirt and a pair of jeans. Owen couldn't help but notice her body. Whoa . . . all right. You're married. She knows that. No funny business. Look at this for what it is—an opportunity. Just . . . just keep a little standoffish so she knows it's all business. What would Pitchford do? Actually, that was a terrible thought—don't do what Pitchford would do!

"Hey. Sam, I want to thank you for agreeing to talk with me. I know you're, uh . . . preoccupied with the tournament but if I could just run some ideas by you."

"Whaddya wanna eat?"

Owen was not sure she had heard a word he'd said. She was studying a menu.

"Anything is fine with me."

"Do you do sushi?"

"Yeah, I could put away some sushi."

"That's what I like to hear. Nice outfit, by the way. You moon-lighting at a Best Buy?"

Owen glanced in the entry mirror. Sure enough, he hadn't even realized he was wearing a blue polo with khakis. What a schlub. He decided to play the part.

"Just let me know if you need anything. The computers in aisle 14 are all 20 percent off."

"Yeah, what kind of processors do they have?"

"They have these ones made by Sparksys—pretty good but not as good as they once were."

"You know, I've always had a thing for men in uniform."

"Well . . . yep."

Owen couldn't think of a comeback. That had escalated quickly.

"I'm just messing with you, Owen. Hold on." Sam called room service and ordered sushi.

"Whaddya want to drink?"

"Water is fine."

Pause.

"Sparkling or regular?"

"Doesn't really matter."

Owen sat down on the small couch facing the bed as Sam finished ordering.

"You know what, bring one of both—and a bottle of sake. The small bottle, the 350-milliliter one, you know what I'm talking about. Cold. I don't care which one. Yep. Room 1108."

Owen smiled. He liked strong women, and Sam's ordering somehow made him feel more at ease—she talked like she was one of the guys. He also noticed that the curtains were open. Another good sign that she wasn't planning on anything inappropriate.

Sam went to the mini-bar and grabbed a bottle of Jack Daniel's for Owen and a water for herself. She sat on the edge of the bed.

"Okay Owen. Let me ask you. You're a married man with a business, right? So why are you here tonight? One of the two must be failing."

"You know which, Sam."

"Or both. But the business is failing for sure, right?"

"It's not failing. It's . . . well . . . here's why I'm here. I spoke with my wife, Lisa, earlier. Sales are down this week. Abysmal. But here's the kicker—our site stats are fantastic yet again. And our PR campaign is just killing it. We just had a new piece on the Outdoor Life Network."

"None of that means anything, Owen. You keep telling me about these **vanity metrics**—the press coverage, the site visits, all that stuff—it all **makes you feel good, but it doesn't really measure anything useful. It doesn't really depict the health of your company**. It doesn't answer the question of whether your big idea can ever become a successful business."

"I agree somewhat. It's . . . ."

"No, Owen. Don't agree somewhat. Agree! I'm so tired of hearing you reference this stuff. None of it matters!"

Was that venom in her tone? Her face was getting red. Sam had moved over to the couch and was getting in his personal space. This was getting intense. For the first time, he noticed how green her eyes were. An uncommon but attractive eye color.

"So what matters, Sam?"

"The most fundamental question for any new idea: do people want it?"

What is she talking about? "Doesn't that just depend on how well you market?"

"It used to. But it doesn't anymore. See, it used to be that companies would build things and then convince people to buy their products. That was back in the day when people actually paid attention to the commercials on TV and there was only one evening newscast and everyone watched it. Today, people are oversaturated with things trying to get their attention, so it's that much harder to convince them to do anything they aren't already interested in doing."

"So how do you convince them?"

"That's just it, Owen. The way to get their attention, **the way to start a successful company, is to solve problems that your customers are already experiencing rather than try to convince them that a problem exists**."

Owen leaned back in retreat and thought for a moment. "What makes you think I didn't do that?"

Sam smiled. "Your sales, Owen. It's pretty obvious that your potential customers don't see the same thing you see."

"Okay, with all due respect, this is nuts. Every business has to market its products to its customers. I was careful to select my target market, and I'm selling them something very similar to what they are already buying. I'm just charging a lot less without compromising on quality."

"I know that sounds like a really logical argument, but the problem is that human beings aren't logical. They are totally irrational, and you can't really predict their behavior, even with such a small modification to an existing product. Everything you planned out for this company, everything you wrote in your business plan, is just a guess. It's a 20-something-page document filled with guesses."

Owen couldn't figure out Sam's angle. He was slightly angry that she was being so condescending. He finished his little bottle of Jack and got another one without asking—if she was going to be disdainful, then she could afford the $6.50 hit.

"Sam, companies have to make predictions and plans. I'm not inventing this concept. It's how the world works."

"Right, existing companies can make predictions and plans because they have historic data, but you have a startup. You're in Wild Wild West territory. Look, do you think I could have written a business plan for playing in the World Series of Poker?"

"What do you mean?"

"Do you think I could have written a business plan where I describe each possible hand and how I'm going to play it when it comes up?"

"Yeah. Okay, Sam."

"Why not? Why would that be a bad idea? Come on. Humor me."

"Because—and I feel like an idiot for saying this—but because it's poker. You know as well I do that you can't possibly know the way one hand is going to play, much less hundreds and thousands of hands."

"And there's more to it than playing hands, right?" her tone was becoming less derisive and slightly more professorial. "You can't predict what the other players are going to do. Human beings are totally irrational. And they don't often act in predictable patterns. Each player here is unique, and each one would play the exact same hand differently. You can only find patterns through interacting with the individual players. You have to read them and their game, you know, learn their mannerisms."

Of course, all of this made sense to Owen, but he had no idea how it related to ReBicycle.

Sam didn't wait for him to ask any questions. She continued: "Well, your idea for ReBicycle is just like this tournament, Owen. It depends on a lot of irrational human beings. And **you just can't predict how these irrational human beings will act**. A lot of statements that you declared as facts in your business plan are just plain guesses about human behavior, and **you can't really declare guesses to be facts without first interacting with your customers to figure out if you're right or wrong**. You can't do well in a tournament without paying attention to the other players, and you can't launch a successful product without understanding who your customers are or what problem you're solving for them."

Owen stifled a yawn; nope, didn't stifle it enough.

"Oh, you're getting bored, Owen? All right. Enough of the niceness." The professor was gone and the scary lady was back. "Let me take a guess. You said last night that you worked for some consulting firm. I bet you were hot shit there. I bet there was a ton of trust fund kids with the right last names who didn't have to work too hard and you were able to lap them in circles."

She was right. He had always stood out at the top of his peer group in the consulting world, and that's why he thought running his own thing would be pretty easy. He had learned from the mistakes of so many giants.

"So take my advice and go back to that consulting firm. Go back to running laps. Because you may have that skill set. But you definitely do not have the skill set to launch a company. Being a great employee or a smart business consultant has nothing to do with starting a business. And this conversation . . . the last conversation . . . every conversation we've had shows me that you are too full of yourself to understand the most fundamental idea of a startup: **it's not about creating a great solution and hoping the market adopts it; it's about understanding your customers first and creating something that adds value to their lives**. Because right now, nobody values your bikes. That's the truth. Sorry. Sales don't lie."

Ouch.

"But I am providing something, Sam!"

"Oh yeah? What world problem are you solving with ReBicycle?"

"What world problem? I'm not curing cancer or anything, but look, there are tons of people in this country, in this hotel probably, who like riding. Like cycling. But don't want to spend a fortune on a high-quality bike. If they knew just how good a quality bike they get could—"

Sam lunged forward and covered his mouth with her hand.

"Shhh. Answer me this, Einstein," unmuzzling him and leaning back to her half of the little couch. How do you know that's a problem?"

"Because I know the bike market. Don't you think I did the research? There is nowhere—and I mean nowhere short of some shady individuals on eBay or Craigslist—where a person can get a bike of my quality at anywhere near our price. You prove me wrong and I'll play the rest of this tournament naked."

Uh-oh. That was a little too sexual. Inadvertently so. Did she notice? Screw it—she couldn't prove him wrong. His research was tight. He watched Sam move to the mini-bar. He looked down at his drink. Two Jacks before dinner. He needed to slow down. Fortunately, it looked as if Sam had calmed down a little. Damn, she got ferocious quick. But so could he. She grabbed another water and flopped down lengthways on the bed.

"Let's recock," she offered in a tone somewhere between professorial and ferocious. "Think of this as a therapy session. You're not the first failing entrepreneur—no offense—I've talked to. I'm helping you out. I'm sure you know the bike market inside and out. That's not your problem, obviously. You sell bikes. Other than that, I have no idea what your company does, nor do I frankly really care, but I'd be willing to bet that the reason you're stuck is that you decided to go all-in on this idea before you were ready. Your idea still has at least one or two major flawed assumptions. Some of your guesses were wrong, Owen! Period. And you don't know which ones. If you've got a weak foundation for a business, you can execute, execute, execute, and it's never going to matter—you can't build a company based on a weak foundation."

"What flawed assumptions?"

"You're assuming your product has value, but you really don't know for sure. Pretty much that defensive act and getting all excited. That shows me that you know the research but you haven't gone out there and talked to potential customers. In fact, the only concrete evidence you seem to have is your sales figures, which prove that something in your assumptions is definitely wrong."

Sam seemed to be in full professor mode now, and she sat up and leaned against the headboard so she could talk with her hands.

"In an ideal world, before you quit your job or sank your life savings into this company, you would have proven whether people actually wanted to buy your products. Now that you are already pot committed, you have to figure out why they don't. You need to go out and talk to your customers. Figure out if they agree with all the assumptions you made in your business plan. Do they think price is important? Will they buy bikes online? Whatever other assumptions are important to your business model. **Put your customers and their needs before your vision for a solution**, Owen. That's one of the most important skills I learned at Sparksys. It's your number-one job in a startup."

A knock.

"Food is here. Hope you're still hungry."

Chapter 9

Don't Gamble—Use Small Bets to Find Opportunities

O wen was fun. Sam had decided that. She could mess with him and he'd take it but also give it back—that was good. He was also nice to look at. Thin, sure, and yeah, he was married, but he didn't really talk about his wife. And more than all of that, he was a good distraction. Listening to his problems had saved her from boredom. And from drinking—she didn't count the little bottle of Sake. And also from psyching herself out for the next day of play. Not that she was really psyched out, but distraction was good. He was a distraction.

She could afford to think about Owen now. To take a quick breather. By mid-afternoon, Sam had the largest chip pile at her table. And the next table and the table after that. There was even a good possibility she was one of the chip leaders in the tournament. It had been a very, very good morning.

She'd knocked out two players in the first hour, one of which was apparently an up-and-coming pro. There had been several audible groans when she knocked him out—most likely financial supporters. If he were smart, the pro had spread his risk among several backers; otherwise, his 10 grand and his 40,000 in chips she'd taken were all his loss. If he were really smart, he'd quit poker because Sam had put him on chasing an open-ended straight as soon as the flop came down and had bet accordingly. And by accordingly she meant bet enough chips to drive him out of the hand. He didn't leave, though. He raised.

The turn featured a jack, giving Sam two pairs, but that really didn't matter. At this point, cards were secondary. She was reading the player. The pro still nodded along to his headphones. God, she hated headphones. She checked this time, forcing him to make an all-in bet. He hesitated for a couple of seconds. That's when she knew. He wouldn't have hesitated if he had it. Sam called his all-in bluff. Sure enough, suited face cards. A total pro hand to play. This time it cost him. He simply misread Sam and her ability to call his bluff.

It was a common encounter for Sam. She knew exactly what went on in that tiny brain of his. He told himself that he would overpower this weak, scared woman with his big bets, and his mind just wouldn't let him see the fact that Sam was a savvy player. He, like many poker players, just equated gender with a set of inherent abilities and motivations. He assumed incorrectly. Sam wished Owen had been there for this hand. She thought through how she would explain her win to him in a way to reaffirm their talk last night.

"You see how this guy just assumed that he could overpower me with his bets? With no evidence so far in the game to support that? He tried to predict my behavior based on what he thought about women or perhaps some previous encounters he's had. That's like trying to predict how customers will react to your product based on how they use other products. It's impossible to do accurately without interacting with those customers to figure out if your assumption was right or wrong."

In this scene she imagined, Owen would thank her profusely for the invaluable advice and ask what he could ever do to repay her for this newfound knowledge. For some reason he was shirtless. Weird.

Sam's second knockout of the morning was of an overmatched amateur. It was notable because it was a woman and the first time Sam had ever knocked another woman player out of the tournament. She felt bad about it. Well, she told herself she felt bad about it. The chips all counted the same. Now she was in a position where she could bully, where she could wait for players whose stacks had dwindled and they only had a couple of times around the table before the blinds knocked them out. She could force them to play with almost no sizable loss to her own stack. She called these the small bets.

Small bets were fun. She could afford to play more hands against them because no single loss would take her out of the tournament, but she knew that their low chip count meant that they were poor players—or opportunities for her to accumulate more chips.

Another small-bet player was fiddling with his few remaining chips, and Sam's attention was brought back to the table. Must be getting close to his all-in bet. Where is he? Two away from the small blind. So that's four hands to possibly play. Which one is he going to choose? She got her answer when he called the bet. Sam looked at her 8-jack off-suit. Ehh . . . why not? It's only eight grand. She called. Three other players called as well—she wasn't the only one who could smell blood in the water. The flop came down and included a 9 and a queen, which gave her a shot at an inside straight.

The other two players checked before the third raised 20 grand. Not worth it. She'd let someone else take the pot. This small bet just turned into a dangerous gamble. The cards weren't as strong as they had been earlier. Short of chasing several rabbit trails, Sam could fold and cruise into the second day. A younger Sam might have kept the foot on the pedal, but something was in the air. Other players could feel the day coming to an end and were starting to act irrationally. That was scary for a chip leader. She took a deep breath. No sense spending good money after bad.

She wouldn't let herself get sucked into this hand. Though she still had a chance of winning, she'd be gambling at this point and hoping to get lucky, and she knew full well that **winning at this tournament wasn't about luck, it was about reducing the number of times she had to get lucky**. She wasn't going to gamble today.

Sam got up from the table. She went to the bathroom and stared in the mirror as she reapplied her lip balm. A bolt suddenly went through her body. She'd made it to the second day! Maybe this is the year she gets to the money. Easy, Sam. Don't get ahead of yourself now. Don't psych yourself out. She started to monitor her breathing, but she could feel the energy.

In the words of Ice Cube, today was a good day. She was rocking the tournament. She didn't have to play tomorrow, so she could relax and catch up with some Vegas friends. Yes, today was a good day. She didn't even have to use her A.K. Maybe Ice Cube had meant ace-king. Damn, that was pretty good, too. Sam was proud of herself.

Her phone vibrated. Owen was calling.

Chapter 10

Even Experts Need to Prepare for New Terrain

Of course, he made assumptions! Who didn't make assumptions? Sam had some good ideas, but jeez, was she on a high horse. Yes, Sparksys was successful. But if it was so successful, why did she sell it? Fridges full of beer and take your dog to work day may do wonders for employee morale, but did she ever have any consulting firms look at her business? Who knew how long Sparksys would last? Whether micro-nano-whatever processors would be replaced next year or the year after that? A hundred years from now people would still be riding bikes. Owen knew that. That wasn't an assumption; that was a damned fact. He was riding one right now.

He was also regretting the ride. It wasn't just the heat. He could tell he was still dehydrated from the Jack Daniel's. All right, no more

Jack Daniel's on this trip. Nothing stronger than beer. No more Sam and no more Jack Daniel's. Is high gear up or down on this bike?

Las Vegas doesn't really have an outskirts. There's the city and then there's desert. It hadn't taken Owen long to find the latter. The roads were narrow, which he didn't like, but traffic was light, so it wasn't too bad. The bike he rented, though, was a piece. Must have weighed 20 pounds. He tried to talk the kid into giving him something better, but this was their demo—come back later and talk to the manager if you want to try something else. Owen knew he couldn't come back later. Stupid bike shop. Wonder how many bikes they sell. If there was any justice in the world, they'd sell only like . . .

Downshift . . . shit! Sand! Shit shit shit! Clip out. Oh shit. Oh . . .

Owen had spaced and not noticed the orange cones on the road. The gravel had turned to dirt and sand, and he needed to get back to his left to get on the pavement over the lip, but now he'd slowed down too much . . . Nope! He was going to bite it. Clip out right clip!

He must have twisted the wrong way. His right leg was caught on the pedal and as he braced for impact, he tried one last time to twist out but succeeded only in turning the bike around halfway and sliding on his right side. His hip hit the edge between the gravel and the dirt/sand and took some of the impact of his knee and elbow. Some, but not all.

It was all over as soon as it happened. Owen lay still for a second, breathing deep with the bike still on top of him. What had just happened? He crashed and skidded. Was he okay? Wiggle toes and fingers. So far, so good. Left elbow already felt sore. Must have come down pretty hard on that. Was he still clipped in? No. Right leg was free. Okay, let's stand up.

As Owen tried to take his first step, a bolt of pain shot to his right knee. He surveyed the damage again. There was a little blood on his shirt, so he must be bleeding on the arm. The knee was really bloody. Hip had a six-inch strawberry below his riding shorts that was slightly oozing blood. He tried to remember if it was next to the second or third orange cone when he'd started sliding. Either way, he skidded at least 10 feet. That was pretty bad. All right. Take another step. Slowly this time. Feel it out.

The jolt returned as soon as Owen lifted his knee. Nope. Not happening. He sat down on the side of the road. He wasn't going anywhere. He knew he'd have to get the knee checked out. He knew he couldn't miss play tomorrow. That was the most important thing. He needed to get back to town.

It took five minutes to call Sam. It was her or an ambulance. He didn't want to use the ambulance. If only he had his former medical coverage! His current deductible might as well have been in Monopoly money. Another joy of self-employment. So, yeah, that was out of the question. Maybe a taxi but the driver might not take the bike or, more likely, not take him because he was too bloody. So that left cars that were passing by and Sam. And no cars had passed since he crashed. The sun was turning red. The phone showed 7:30 P.M. Maybe another hour of light. Maybe.

"Hey, Owen, can I call you back?"

"Wait, Sam! No. You can't."

"Why. What's up?"

"Hey. Long story short. I've been in a bicycle accident. I'm somewhere in the middle of the Vegas desert. Google Map says about 14 miles out. Can't walk. I'm bloody. The bike is . . ."

"Where are you?"

"Can you come pick me up?"

"Where are you?"

"I thought you'd rented a car . . ."

"Owen. Just tell me where the hell you are."

"Looks to be about a quarter-mile north of where Belo Drive intersects Belton Road."

"Okay. I'm coming. You okay?"

"Thanks, Sam. I'll be okay. Thanks."

She didn't seem happy about it, but she was coming. She did seem to actually care whether he was okay. He couldn't get over how she could be so callous one minute and yet be so nice the next. Wait, that didn't make sense.

Oooooh, the knee hurt.

Chapter 11

People Don't Buy Visionary Products; They Buy Solutions to Their Problems

I t was dark. Owen felt dark. He must have been more than 14 miles out. The ride back was taking forever. He was avoiding any eye contact with Sam. He was trying to pretend that looking out the window at a dark desert was the most exciting thing to do. After he answered the basic questions—Are you all right? Yes. Do you need to go to a hospital? No. Where do you want to go? The hotel.—Sam could tell he didn't want to talk and had let him be.

That hour in the desert that Owen spent waiting for her had given him time to think. A lot of time to think. The kind of thinking he hadn't sat down and done since he opened ReBicycle.

At first, he thought about calling Lisa, but it wasn't like she could do anything, and he didn't want her to worry. He told himself that was the primary reason he didn't call her. The real reason wasn't quite so unselfish. He knew that if he called Lisa, he'd have to explain how he was getting back, that a woman he had only just met was driving all the way out to the desert to pick him up. Not that he had done anything wrong, but the pain in his knee was bad enough and he didn't feel capable of tiptoeing through that minefield of a conversation.

He was feeling sorry for himself. He hadn't allowed himself to feel that way in a long time. It felt good. Like a release. There was no crying, but he wouldn't have been against tears.

His mind raced. Images of Lisa, Gary, the whole team—how they would take the news of ReBicycle's shutting down. The more he looked at the problem, the more it pointed right back to him. Bottom line, he had failed them. Turns out, he wasn't as smart or talented as he thought. He couldn't figure it out. He just couldn't work his way out of it. He had just thrown all that money away. Money he wasn't getting back. And, according to Sam, it seems as though he had been doomed to fail from the very beginning.

They rode on in silence. Sam didn't flip on the radio, which Owen found weird. But still, the silence didn't bother him. It didn't seem to bother her. They were comfortable in silence. That usually takes a long time, so Owen found that weird, too. Finally, Owen spoke.

"I think I'm going to close it down."

"What?"

"ReBicycle. I think . . . well . . . I was lying on the side of that road, Sam, and it suddenly hit me. It just came to me. This crash. This crash is ReBicycle. This crash is my business. I was doing something I love—I was riding—and it bit me. I got hurt doing it. That's not any different than my business. And I was thinking, at what point do I realize that I don't have the answers and stop the skidding? It's been a year already. I clearly don't have the marketing skills to sell these bikes, or there's something wrong with the design. I don't know, but how long do I wait to figure it out? What? Two years. Three years? I'm ready to stop skidding. Win or lose at this tournament, I'm going to dust myself off and get up from this crash. From ReBicycle."

Silence.

More silence.

Finally, "You know what your problem is, Owen?"

"What?"

"You haven't learned anything from this experience."

Owen scoffed loudly. "What are you talking about?"

"ReBicycle. You haven't figured out that **companies don't go out of business because they fail to build a product. Companies go out of business because they fail to build anything that people want**."

"So you're saying I didn't market it right?"

Sam shook her head from side to side ferociously, and then just let out a loud grunt. Owen had no idea why she was getting so upset, but before he could try to figure it out, he felt the car take a sharp right turn into an empty parking lot.

"What are you doing?"

Sam didn't answer. She stopped the car just as quickly as she had turned, and before Owen knew it, she had violently flung open her door and got out. She briskly made her way to Owen's side of the car. She didn't even bother to open his door, she just shouted through the glass.

"Get out of the car, Owen!"

He wasn't sure what was going on. Was she planning on leaving him here? What did he say to set her off?

"Get out of the car!" She shouted.

Owen obliged. Slowly. Everything ached. Best to stay close to the car and use it prop himself up if need be. Sam was pacing around. Here he was, thinking she was going to talk him off a ledge, and now it seemed as if she was the one who'd gone off the ledge. Finally, she looked at him.

"You are no different than every other first-time entrepreneur. You think you're a visionary. You think that you found something no one else could see and you were going to work on it and make it perfect and give it to the world. And once a few people saw your vision, they'd see what was missing this whole time, and they would tell everyone they knew, and you would sell millions!"

She was pacing around and gesturing with her hands, "Owen, **people don't buy visionary products. People buy solutions to their problems!**"

"And you don't think ReBicycle solves a problem?"

No answer. Sam stomped over to the trunk of the car, opened it, and started fumbling with something inside, maybe her purse? Whatever she was doing, it sounded like she was looking for something she couldn't find. She pulled out a backpack and started digging for something. Her arm went still when it had found its target. "Here we go."

She pulled out a pack of Camels that looked like they had rain damage.

"These things gotta be at least six months old. I smoked all through college before giving it up. When I started Sparksys, well, with the stress and everything . . . what? You want one?"

Owen hadn't smoked a cigarette since . . . since . . . it had to be high school, trying to look cool. Oh, what the hell.

"Sure."

Owen took a cigarette but just felt awkward. The opposite of cool. He had a quick moment of self-clarity, 30-plus years old and smoking outside a closed office supply store in some bland Vegas suburb . . . this was not how he had pictured life after the consulting world. Sam lit her cigarette. She didn't offer Owen a light. He didn't ask for it, either. She didn't seem to care one way or the other. He could tell that she was working up something to say.

"People don't buy products, Owen." Puff. He could tell she was trying to control her vigor. The cigarette seemed to help. "They buy solutions to their problems. So **if your business is failing from the get-go, it means that either**"— puff; she held up a single finger—"**you built a solution for a problem that doesn't exist, or**"—she held up a second finger—"**your customers don't know they have the problem or it's not important enough that they are willing to pay money to solve it, or**"— she put up a third finger—"**your solution doesn't actually solve the problem**. Those are the only options." A long drag. She was enjoying that cigarette way too much. "So let me ask you, Owen, why do people want your product?"

"Well, there's just no other place people can buy bikes of this quality for the prices we are able to offer. I've looked . . ."

"So the price? You think the price of road bikes is a problem?"

Owen tried not to roll his eyes. What a stupid question. "Yeah, of course, people want a more affordable option than what they can find at a bike store."

"What people?"

"What do you mean? People who buy bicycles."

"Like all bike shoppers?"

"I mean, who wouldn't want a better deal on their bike purchases? It's just common sense."

"Owen, that's the problem right there." She took a final drag of her cigarette and threw it to the ground. "You have no idea if people who buy bikes think price is a problem. You thought that made perfect sense and you started your company, hired people, whatever, based on *that* assumption. Why? Because you didn't think it was a risky assumption. But it is! Every assumption is a risky assumption when you are interacting with human beings. I'm irrational. You're irrational. We're smoking—what's rational about putting tar in your lungs? Everybody is irrational, and they don't necessarily buy things just because they are cheap. Or maybe they do. But the point is, you don't know. And you spent a lot more time thinking about your vision, the bikes, and the web site and production, and not enough time thinking about the customers and their problems. It's not about what the bikes look like, how you brand them, how you market them. At least it's not about that when you first start your company. Before any of that will ever matter, you need to understand why your customers would want ReBicycle. That ReBicycle solves some sort of serious problem or adds value to their lives. That is the foundation."

Finally, Sam tossed Owen the lighter. Actually lighting the cigarette still felt cool. Being hunched over in pain . . . not so much.

"But price is always a factor, Sam."

"Maybe it's a factor. You're assuming again. And just because it's one factor doesn't make it a migraine-level problem."

"What do you mean?" The cigarette tasted awful, but he wouldn't allow his face to betray him.

"Not every problem will do, Owen. **You will significantly increase your chances of startup success if you focus on solving only those problems that are causing serious issues for your customers**. Customer problems are either headaches or migraines. Your ordinary headache is just something annoying. 'Oh, I have a headache,' and maybe you take an aspirin or maybe you don't. Either way, it goes away and you don't even remember it an hour later."

Sam got out another cigarette and reached for the lighter, "I take my dog, Thatcher, on a lot of walks, and I have to pick up after him, after he . . . you know . . . does his thing. It's annoying. And I wish I didn't have to do it. If you asked me if picking up after my dog is a problem, I would say yes! But I'm not going to spend any money on a fancy pooper scooper that I have to bring with me on my walks. My current solution, used bags from the grocery store, works well enough, and I honestly have never gone online to look for other options. As problems go, it's just like a headache. It's annoying, but short of taking some over-the-counter medicine, the majority of people wouldn't do anything else to treat it."

Owen wasn't sure where she was going with this and why they couldn't just talk in the car. He figured he'd subtly remind her of his condition. "You got any aspirin in that backpack?"

Sam shook her head. Owen couldn't help noticing that the obnoxious red lighting of the "Office Depot" sign lit her face. She was awfully pretty. Even when angry. She was preaching again.

"And then there's migraine problems . . . Jesus! Have you ever had a migraine?"

"No, but I've seen the commercials."

"The commercials can't even begin to explain it. They are horrible! The pain is like an icepick in your brain. A little elf with an ice pick." She mimicked an elf picking away at something. "With most pain you can lie down or do something to make the pain bearable. With a migraine there is no escaping. The world is blurry and your stomach is churning. Oh God, they're awful. And some of them last for days or weeks."

"Something you have a lot of personal experience with?"

"Not too much. Thank God. I hate even thinking of them. That's how you know it's a migraine—if thinking about the problem causes a problem. Chronic migraines. That's a problem worth solving. Hence the commercials. Hence the drugs and billboards on the side of the road advertising doctors who treat them with everything, including brain surgery. From the handful of migraines I've had, I can tell you, on a scale of 1 to 10, the pain is a 10. A throbbing 10."

She stared at Owen as if trying to gauge whether he was coming to some sort of epiphany. It was as though she was literally waiting for a cartoon light bulb to illuminate over his head. When she didn't see whatever she was looking for, she continued, "So last month Thatcher got really sick. He was vomiting every few hours and couldn't keep anything down. He kept looking at me with these puppy-dog eyes, trying to communicate to me that something was wrong and he wasn't feeling well. After like 20 hours of this, I rushed him to the vet's office to get him checked out. This was a migraine problem, Owen. It didn't matter what tests the doctor wanted to run, or what prescription he wanted to issue, I would pay anything and everything to make Thatcher feel better."

She seemed to look again for the light bulb over Owen's head, and when it wasn't there, she pressed forward. "So, let me ask you this, Owen. On the pain scale, where is price for people buying bicycles? You solving a problem that rates a 10 on the pain scale? I guarantee you it's not that bad or bike shops would be going out of business right and left!"

He didn't know how to respond. Sam leaned down to the pavement and stubbed out her cigarette. "I'm cold. And hungry. You want to get something to eat?"

Chapter 12

Only Customers Can Tell You if You've Found a Problem Worth Solving

Sam felt bad about losing her temper on the car ride. She had driven all the way out to the middle of Area 51 or wherever the hell to get Owen, and he just started spouting off all this nonsense she'd heard a million times from first-time entrepreneurs. Something just snapped. Yeah, he was in pain and looked pretty bad, but the knee didn't look broken to her and while she wasn't Dr. Quinn, Medicine Woman, even she could see the elbow definitely wasn't broken. She couldn't help herself. It was as though she wasn't just yelling at Owen, but all the entrepreneurs who operated under similarly flawed assumptions.

As much as she didn't like to admit it to herself, Sam knew she had a soft spot for Owen. In a lot of ways, he was a lot like her ex-husband, Stephen. Definitely passionate, maybe a little misguided, but he was well intentioned. He could have definitely made a move in her hotel room, but he hadn't.

Oh, jeez. The Florence Nightingale effect was taking place. She was feeling sorry for him now, too. Giving him excuses. He's a grown man, Sam! He's got people depending on him making the right decisions. Don't soften up. Don't worry about telling him like it is. You can only help.

"So what would you have done differently, Sam?"

"I'm sorry?" It seemed like Owen was getting ready for round two of the previous fight. Sam was happy to talk business all night, but she was hoping for a few minutes to enjoy her angel hair pasta. Oh well.

"If you were in my shoes, when ReBicycle was just getting off the ground, what would you have done differently?

Yep. More shop talk. Screw the angel hair. At least she could enjoy the martini . . . and the next one. "You know why we're here in Vegas playing in the World Series of Poker rather than the World Series of slot machines, Owen?"

"Why?"

"Because it takes skill to win at poker and just luck to win at slot machines. We're not here hoping to get lucky." She punctuated "get lucky" with a wink. "We're here to use our skills to reduce the need for luck and play the other players, not the cards."

"Okay, Sam, so how does that apply to ReBicycle?"

"It's a complete parallel, Owen. If I were starting the company from scratch, I would do whatever I needed to do to take the need for luck out of the equation and reduce my risk of failure. I would prove that people wanted my product before I went all-in on the idea."

"And how would you do that?"

"Okay, here's what you did. You came up with the idea for ReBicycle and quickly started building it, the bikes, the web site, all of these things that take a lot of time and money to create."

"That's an understatement."

"Then you branded ReBicycle, you came up with marketing materials, started going after PR. This took a significant amount of time and money, too."

Owen nodded.

"And finally, you went out looking for customers. Unfortunately, you didn't find them, and you probably thought something was wrong with the initial idea. So you went back to the drawing board and redesigned something, what was it? Something about the bike? The web site?"

"We put up a new web site." He said slowly. Sam could see that she had his attention.

"Right, and the customers still didn't come. This is crazy. You're stuck in this loop that you keep repeating over and over expecting something different to happen at the end, but what you really need to change is the order. So if I were starting ReBicycle from scratch, I'd start with the idea, but then I would immediately want to make sure I had a customer—before I spent any time or money on building or branding."

Owen, despite his obvious wounds and the fact that he was sitting in a restaurant wearing biker shorts, appeared to be listening for the first time, so she kept going.

"So, **before I did anything, and I mean anything else**, like picking a name, creating legal documents, raising money, or quitting my job, I'd work to figure out: **who is my customer, what is their problem, and will they buy my product to solve their problem**?"

"Because people don't buy products—they buy solutions to their problems, right?" A smirk from Owen. Either he was making fun of her and her little rant in the Office Depot parking lot, or finally, something might have snuck through his road rash and into his brain. Probably a little bit of both—like part gin and part vermouth.

"Yep." Sam raised her glass in a mock toast to Owen. "**And you can't answer any of those questions on your own. Only**

through interactions with your customers. They are the only ones who can answer these questions for you."

"So how would you do that? Figure out the problem?"

"You need to find out if the high price of road bikes is a big problem. And who it's a problem for. I guarantee you it's not everyone who buys bikes. You need to hang out where these people spend their time and talk to 100, 150 people." She swirled a large heap of pasta onto her fork. "Something like that. People you don't know and people who don't know what you're looking for. It's a bunch of legwork, but then you'd find out how many mention price. Because right now you don't know. Like, if you had to guess, how many out of 100 bike aficionados, enthusiasts, whatever, would you say list price as their most important selection criteria?" She took her big bite. God, this was good.

"It's got to be something like 50 percent, Sam." Owen hadn't even touched his plate of food yet.

"And how do you know? You don't really. Fifty percent is incredible if that's the case. I bet the real number is lower. Like a lot lower. Like if 25 percent thought price was the most important part of their bike, then you and I wouldn't be here right now, enjoying this unbelievable pasta." He didn't take the hint and kept ignoring his plate.

"Here's where you're wrong, Sam. You keep talking about talking to people. But I did that. When I first got started."

"Nope. Doesn't count. Guarantee you were in sales mode. You already knew what you wanted to create. You were the visionary, remember? So either they lied to you about what was important because they wanted to spare your feelings, or you didn't hear honest feedback when you got it."

She pointed at him with her fork, flinging a few small pieces of angel hair. "You have to **take yourself out of sales mode when trying to identify your customer and their problem**. Your objective should be to learn, like you are a detective. Like someone who is testing a theory. Like a negative result is just as valuable as a positive. The worst thing you could get is a false positive because that would just waste more of your resources moving forward."

She had his attention. At least she thought she did. It was darn sure the pasta didn't. Still hadn't touched it. She reached her fork over and helped herself to his food. Chicken Madeira. A little too heavy on the sauce. "Here's what you've got to do. . . ."

She picked up her martini glass and pulled out the napkin underneath. It felt dry enough to write on. With her left hand, Sam fished around in her purse for a pen. Where's a good whiteboard when you need one?

"Well, first, we have to **clearly articulate the idea in a way that describes its value.**"

She scribbled on the napkin.

I will help (customers) solve (problem) by (solution)

"The shorter your descriptions for customer, problem, and solution, the better. So let's try it. Lets fill in the blanks for ReBicycle. Go ahead."

Owen looked at the napkin. "I will help people who buy bicycles."

"Wait right there, Owen. Not just people who buy bicycles, right? Because people who shop for Huffys at Target aren't going to care about your product, so it's got to be a specific group of people. Remember, this isn't the last thing your business will ever do; it's only the first thing. So you aren't thinking about the first million customers, just the first 10 or 100 customers, and the more specific you can make these descriptions, the easier it will be for you to find these people and test your assumptions."

"Okay, I will help people who shop at specialty bike stores . . ." He looked at her for approval. While chewing a massive bite of food, Sam gave him a thumbs-up to let him know he was on the right track, so he continued, ". . . solve the problem of expensive bicycles by . . ."

She swallowed and put her hands up in a time-out pose. "I'm going to interrupt you just really quick to say, we have to be just as specific about the problem as we were about the customer. And you have to say it in a way that doesn't sell people on a problem but could be proven right or wrong."

He nodded and tried again. "So, the problem of not wanting to pay retail for a quality road bike by . . ." he glanced back at the napkin, "by . . ." Owen struggled with how to phrase this. "By letting them . . . by providing an online store where they can buy quality refurbished bicycles at half the price of new bikes at those retail locations."

"Perfect! Great job, Owen. Okay, let's write that down before I forget it." She scribbled on her napkin underneath her initial directions.

I will help (customers) solve
(problem)   by   (solution)

Owen will help people who shop
at specialty bike stores Solve the
problem of not wanting to pay retail
for a quality road bike By providing
an online store where they can
buy quality refurbished bicycles at
half the price of new bikes at
those retail locations.

"Okay, so that's your initial idea. And like I've been telling you, you can't move forward on it until you can prove that there are customers who want to buy it. There are two parts to this equation. First, you have to prove that the customer and the problem exist."

"You sound a lot like me from my consulting days." He was starting to look less skeptical of her than he had in the previous few days.

"I'll take that as a compliment." She flipped over the napkin and prepared to write again. "Okay, so we need to confirm that you've found a problem worth solving by answering the following questions."

I know I have a Problem
Worth Solving because:
1. My customers are _____.
2. Their problem is _____.
3. They are currently solving
   their problem by _____.
4. They have tried other solutions
   in the past by _____.
5. On a scale of 1-10, the
   seriousness of the problem is __.
6. They would spend $_____
   to fix this problem.

"See how there's nothing about the solution on here yet?"

"Yeah."

"That's on purpose. The problem and the solution are totally independent of one another. First, you have to prove that the problem exists, that it's a serious problem that amounts to a migraine. Then we can worry about whether customers will actually buy your product as a solution. Make sense?"

"Well, when you put it that way . . ."

"Don't be flippant. And eat your Madeira. Listen, this stuff is invaluable, Owen. You need to **first and foremost figure out if price is a problem and what customer segment it's a problem for**. And you can't use your own words to answer these questions. You can only use actual statements that you hear your potential customers say when you talk to them. Like, I would go—physically go—to a half-dozen bike shops. Good ones. And interview everyone who goes in there. Not picking and choosing. I mean like everyone. Do that and speak to 100 or so strangers, just to see if price is a migraine-level problem or if it's simply a headache."

The waiter walked by their table and Sam gestured for a second martini.

"Well, I can see how that would have been useful when I first got started." Slight picking at his plate now. Definitely in pain. Ah, he'll live.

"It's not too late, Owen."

"Sam, I'm out of money. Out of time. There's nothing left. It's time to shut it down. I just want to focus on poker now. I want to go back to my hotel room and go to bed and not think of ReBicycle or how it'll never compare to Sparksys. Oh, and this Madeira is terrible."

"Actually, this is probably the best time for you to have these conversations! I mean, you really don't care either way right now, right? You can learn how this process works, and if you ever want to start another company, you can do it the right way. You can't learn this stuff without practicing it Owen. It's not easy."

"You think I can figure out what went wrong with ReBicycle?"

"Absolutely!" Actually, Sam didn't think it was an absolute. Or even 50 percent. But now was not the time to shine a cold light on a business Owen had never really thought through. The guy was literally beaten down.

"But **you can't rationalize why price is a problem on your own; the only way to answer these questions is through conversations with real people you don't know who actually fit into your customer description**. You can make all the guesses you want about what went wrong, but I promise you, you will learn so much more from these conversations if you follow the rules: no selling, just learning, no talking about any solution, just trying to figure out the problem, and whether it's a headache or a migraine."

Silence. More playing with the Madeira.

"You know how I started Sparksys? I was working as a trade-show model making, like, I don't know, $10 an hour. This was the late '90s, but even then that was still like getting paid in lint and confederate nickels. Now granted, I got to flirt a lot. I enjoyed that. But it wasn't glamorous, especially considering the risk I was taking if people in my master's program found out what I was doing. But you sometimes got per diem. I remember that. It was nice. By this time I'd already had the idea for Sparksys and invested a good amount in it but was just going through the motions—you know, another wanna-be entrepreneur with an idea, and, of course, I had nothing to show for my time or investment. I'd try and set up meetings with Intel, Hewlett-Packard, even Kodak. Nobody wanted to look at my idea."

She leaned forward in her chair to emphasize the next part of her story.

"What ended up working and what saved the company that became Sparksys was my being a trade show model. At electronics shows, I would basically interview businessmen I didn't know. Dozens of them. I'd say my ex-boyfriend thinks he's figured out some way to solve a specific microprocessing problem, but he was so dumb, how did he ever think anyone else had problems with blah blah blah? And the blah, blah, blah was whatever iteration I had for Sparksys at the time. Most of the time the businessmen agreed or didn't listen, or they'd laugh because they were trying to flirt. I remember at a show in Reno I was telling a really smart but dorky guy about my ex-boyfriend's idea, and I described how he thought he figured out the problem of shrinking microprocessors by freezing them near total zero and without any damage to the chip. The guy suddenly got really quiet and started peppering me with questions."

"Okay."

"That's when I knew, Owen! That was the aha! I had hit a nerve or something. The next 20 conversations went the exact same way. These guys wanted my ex's contact info a lot more than mine all of a sudden. The idea was overriding *this*." She did a mock gesture as if she were still a trade show model, but instead of a car, she was showing off her body. "If they wanted my ex's number more than mine, I knew I was on to something. It was another year or so of work after that, but the gist of that idea is what eventually became Sparksys and what I was able to market to Asus, Acer, and then Dell and even Apple. Those guys were objectively confirming that I had stumbled onto a migraine-level problem! There was nothing in it for them."

"Just like that, huh?"

"I can't tell you how obvious it is when you find a migraine problem. **Once you hit that nerve, they aren't just going to agree with you and walk away. They'll tell you what they are currently doing to try to solve it. All the things they've tried in the past that didn't work. Even how much money they've spent trying to find a solution. When you bring up a migraine problem, you'll see the customer's eyes dilate right in front of you, like you just stuck your finger in a serious wound.** That's where I made my money with Sparksys. **The bigger the pain, the easier it will be to sell the solution.** Plain and simple. You've got to hit a nerve."

"And so I just need to go out there and flirt with a bunch of businessmen at trade shows?"

"You joke, but that's right. Maybe not at trade shows and maybe not flirt. But talk to men, women, anybody that fits your customer description." She pointed to the napkin. "Listen first and then talk. I can't stress that enough. Just **remember to listen. Don't load questions. Don't sell them on a problem.** Just listen to random strangers. If they're willing to talk, let 'em talk. Ninety percent of the stuff they say may be crap and boring, but there's always a sliver of value there. As long as they're honest and know you're not try-ing to sell them something. Mark my words—easier said than done. Especially since you don't have boobs and a clipboard. You need to figure out a way to question them not on behalf of ReBicycle but some other nonthreatening party. Someone truly interested in figuring out if there's a business there."

". . . anything more to drink?" The waiter had finally returned.

"Yes. Please, God yes. One more martini for me." Sam said. Thinking about Sparksys had gotten her pumped up again. Way pumped up.

"Yeah, and I'll take a clipboard." Owen was still being sarcastic, but at least he was smiling now. Sam could tell he was getting it. Slowly but surely. Hell, it might even take another fall off the bike, but he was going to get it. Plus his spirits were certainly at their highest all evening. The Chicken Madeira was still untouched.

Chapter 13

Hoping and Praying for Luck Is Not a Strategy

Owen was staring at an ace and queen of clubs. Squinting was more like it. He was still waking up, and it was almost too early to get such a playable hand, especially one he'd have to think about and try to figure out the odds for like the ace-queen. Everything hurt. Everything. To reach for the cards hurt his elbow and shoulder. His right knee was huge. He hadn't iced it until he'd gotten back to his room from the dinner and talk with Sam, and that was—what—2 A.M.?

He was freezing because he was wearing workout shorts. Having denim jeans rub against his leg had been too painful. His head hurt. He barely got any rest. Every time he moved while sleeping, pain jostled him awake. He had dared to try to take a shower, but the damn hotel shower had like a thousand spigots and he couldn't escape the blast so he ended up half-in, half-out, washing what body parts he could still get under the water. The shower had been a bad idea. More than anything, he wanted to crawl into his own bed and to hear Lisa's sympathetic "awww" as she brought him an ice pack.

Ughhh. Lisa. She must be either worried sick or pissed at him for not calling yesterday. But he couldn't call her this morning. It had taken him twice as long to get ready than he planned, and he needed a certain amount of time to explain the accident. He needed to focus now.

It had been only 36 hours since he'd last sat at a poker table, but it felt like a month. Not only was his body in a completely different condition, but so was his mind. At the end of the first day, he hadn't thought about ReBicycle or business or life. Just poker. He had felt focused, charged. When people describe living in the moment, they must mean moments like the end of that first day. Now, he couldn't stop thinking about anything but cards. This was terrible. And that cigarette. Was that a hallucination? Had he really smoked a stupid cigarette? In a big-box parking lot? What an idiot.

Ughhh. Focus. Pray for focus. Pray for good hands. Wait—you've got a good hand. Focus on poker. Focus on ace-queen. Ace-queen suited. Definitely bet before the flop, but not too big. You want some action, but not too much action. Doubling the pot is good, so just make it smooth.

"Raise."

Owen looked to his right. The big blind right next to him raised before he got a chance.

It was the elderly Asian woman who kept referring to herself as the "Dragon Lady" and was also low on chips. Probably trying to protect her blinds and hoping to steal the pot. Owen called.

The flop came down and Owen found a match to his ace. He had top pair with a good kicker. Not a bad hand, especially against a big blind. She likely has mediocre cards and she's trying to hide them with her bets.

"Raise another 20," she said with confidence, but Owen could tell something was amiss. Calling this bet would leave him with just $10,000 in chips, but he knew this woman. He had watched her for the last hour. This was out of character for her. When she had great cards before, she didn't try to muscle people out of the hand. She was acting like someone on tilt. She was getting desperate. She was low on money and taking bigger and bigger gambles with her cards.

"Call." Owen uttered while turning to lock eyes with his opponent.

She's too committed now. Owen could see it in her face. She isn't thinking straight. No matter what card comes out now, she'll go all-in as a last sign of force. He'd seen it enough times to know.

The turn card was a jack. No real threat there. But before the dealer finished putting it down on the table, Dragon Lady eagerly called "all-in."

For some reason, Owen thought back to an old business school lecture with Professor Simons, "Companies on tilt are no longer operating rationally. They are taking greater and greater bets to try to recoup their investment. They are now hoping to get lucky and, ironically, will just end up spiraling to a faster death. You shouldn't gamble in business," he would say. "Your odds of success are incredibly low. Save it for the casinos."

"Call." It was instinct. He didn't need to think about it. Owen and the Dragon Lady flipped over their cards, preparing for the river card. She had an 8-9 off-suit. A complete bluff on her part. There were no cards that could help her now. She knew that she had lost.

The dealer was required to ceremoniously complete dealing the hand, but she had already gathered her Dragon Lady things and was walking away by the time he finished the hand. She had mentally checked out before this hand. She was just hoping to get lucky, which is just as bad of a strategy in poker as it is in business.

All right. Back in business. That was a $60,000 pot! Suddenly, the pain throughout his body didn't seem quite as bad. As Owen collected his winnings and restacked them, he thought about how he would have played the hand if this were the only hand he had ever played against Dragon Lady. He likely would have folded. He would have been nervous to gamble all his money with no information on her playing style, and she did seem confident. That would have likely scared him off. He thought about the benefit of having played with her over the last hour and understanding not only her style but her motivations. He had her pegged.

He flashed back to last night's conversation and Sam telling him that "you can't answer any questions about your customers without understanding them, getting to know them, and figuring out their motivations."

It wasn't hard for Owen to see the parallel. If he spent half as much time with actual customers as he had with the Dragon Lady, he could figure out why they weren't interested in his bikes. He just needed to treat them like one of the other players at the table. Observing them, trying to figure out why they are doing what they are doing. He had never considered observing potential ReBicycle customers; he was always just trying to sell the product. But what could it hurt now?

Right after lunch, Owen had an opportunity to win some serious chips. He had pocket 10s and ended up winning a huge pot with three-way action. He finally had a large stack, around $200,000 in chips. Raking it in felt good. For the first time in a long time, Owen felt validation for his decisions.

About an hour later—with a little room to breathe, thanks to the pocket 10s—he came up with a plan of interviewing potential ReBicycle customers that he thought might work. It was out there and could totally backfire, but, whatever, what happened in Vegas stayed in Vegas. He needed Sam's help.

At the next break, he took an elevator to the 11th floor, and sprinted down the hallway to room 1108. He knocked. Where else would she be?

He waited and knocked again. More waiting, but nothing happened. Owen started walking back to the elevator.

"Hey, Owen."

He turned around. Sam had finally opened the door. She was just wearing a long shirt and no pants and definitely no makeup. Judging by her wild hair and eyes, she'd been asleep.

"What's up, Sam?" He smiled and started walking back toward her door. He took his time, trying not to seem too eager to see her half-naked.

"Hey. How you doing in the tournament? You look rough."

"Yeah, you don't look much better yourself, Sam."

"Shut up." She returned his smile. "You gonna come in?" The invitation took Owen by surprise. She was leaning against the doorframe.

"No." He shook his head.

"Why are you here, then?"

"Okay, Sam. Long story short. I need you to do me a favor. It has to do with last night. Our conversation. I remember reading in a trade mag about there being a high-end bike shop opening in some hotel in town. Maybe Aladdin or Wynn. One of those. Can you help me find that store? And then here's the big favor. Call and find out if there are any managers who are on leave or racing or gone this week?"

"You want me to do what?" She rubbed her eyes. She was still waking up. Clearly, she was of the opinion that the shirt she had on was long enough not to necessitate a pair of pants.

"Sam, I've got $200,000 in chips downstairs, and I have to get back because these breaks are pretty short. I need you to find this bike store and the name of one of the managers who's out or on vacation. That's all."

"Hold on." She rubbed her head. "By when?"

"Just sometime today." He was already walking back to the elevator. "Thank you!"

"You owe me dinner!"

He spun around and, while walking backwards and laughing, shouted, "Okay, but you have to wear pants!" then spun back around and picked up a light jog. Well, it was a fast hobble. As he entered the elevator, he glanced back and noticed Sam was still hanging out her door, facing his direction.

Owen leaned against the back wall of the elevator and smiled. It was less than an hour later that he felt a buzz in his right pocket. It was a text from Sam. "L'Alpe Cyclery. Rio Casino. 2nd Level Basement Floor. The day manager, Chris, is racing in Seattle . . . u owe me."

He texted back: "You're a rock star. Thank you so much!"

Owen laughed to himself just a bit and grinned as he looked down at his lap to make it clear that he wasn't reacting to his current hand. The bike shop was only two floors below the hotel. This wouldn't be so hard after all. He felt another buzz. Another text from Sam.

"Get your bloody bike out of the back of my car!"

Shit. He'd forgotten to return the bike.

Chapter 14

It's Never Too Late to Test Your Assumptions

It was past midnight. Tournament play had wrapped up for the day a few hours ago. The last piece of advice the dealer had imparted to their table before he took off for the night was to get a good night's sleep. Yeah, right. Owen was staring at the hotel room TV, trying to decompress but not having much luck. He just couldn't get to sleep.

He thought he should strategize for day three. That might do the trick—talking about poker instead of playing it always made him sleepy. There was definitely a lot to think about. The speed was quick, and the professionals were starting to pick on weaker players. So far, not Owen. How to keep that from happening—okay, first, think like a good poker player. How could he project strength? What would Sam do?

This wasn't working. He wasn't getting any sleepier. Antsy, yes. Not tired. Owen thought about turning off the reading lamp, but he knew it wouldn't help. His brain was racing too quickly. Time to grab the shoes.

It took Owen some time to find a low-key bar where he could have a beer and set up his computer. Every bar at the hotel seemed like a themed pickup venue. He finally found a wine bar with an open table near the bar.

Owen sat down and opened his computer. He'd work on some nonleading questions. The kind he could use to really learn about his customers rather than trying to convince them of anything.

"Heyyyyy. My name is Marcus J, and I was wondering what flight you'd like to enjoy tonight?"

"Excuse me?"

"My name is Marcus J. I just saw you sit down. We have a celebrity sommelier this evening helping our resident expert, Anna M, pick out wines, and the special flight this evening is a sample of four Riojas from across the Spanish region, all specifically ch—"

"Do you have any beer?"

Marcus J didn't seem to appreciate the interruption. "I can get you a menu."

"Nah. Just give me a pale ale of whatever."

Marcus J got quite curt. Definitely not happy to see Owen wasn't a wine enthusiast. Ah, he'd get over it. Back to work.

Once Owen had finished his first beer, the questions really started flowing . . . well, sort of. At least better than before.

By 1 A.M, Owen had 10 questions typed out. They were good questions, not leading, just trying to figure out what was important to bike purchasers when they were making their decisions and where price ranked on that list. Was it the most important thing? The second most important thing?

As Owen reviewed the questions, making small grammatical changes, his phone buzzed. It was Lisa.

"Hi there."

"Owen! I can't believe you're up!"

"I can't believe *you're* up. Is everything okay?"

"Yeah. Just got home from Mary's bachelorette party. Couldn't sleep."

"What is it, like, 4 A.M. there?"

"Yeah . . ."

Then garble. One of their phones was losing reception. "What?" he asked.

Crystal clear again. "I said it'll be time to wake up soon. Where are you?"

"At the hotel. I couldn't sleep, so I brought my computer down to the bar."

"Sounds pretty loud."

"Does it? This is the quiet one. It's a wine bar."

"Are you sure it's not a wine nightclub?"

"Funny."

"What?" The cell was breaking up again.

"I said funny. Funny. You're funny."

"Can you leave the bar?"

"I was just thinking the same thing. Give me a second."

Owen walked outside the door to one of those ubiquitous benches that every hotel in Vegas has next to the elevators.

"Hey, I just left. Can you hear me? What's up?"

"I was just hoping to hear your voice. What are you up to? Shouldn't you be sleeping?"

"I'm just doing a little work. I don't know. I got this burst of energy. It was a good day."

"Oh yeah? From playing poker?"

"Yeah. That and I met this other player on my first day, a successful entrepreneur actually, and we got to talking about the biz and then last night, during the dinner break, we talked for a long time about what people frequently do wrong when launching a company."

"You mean like ReBicycle?" Lisa asked.

"No. Not 'like ReBicycle.' I mean ReBicycle itself. We talked about how I started with an idea . . . I thought I was some sort of visionary. I thought I could see something no one else had ever picked up on and that I was disrupting a huge market before someone else could figure it out. But you know as well as I do that our initial orders never translated to the volumes of customers we anticipated. And I'm thinking—well, this entrepreneur and I were thinking, brainstorming—that part of it is because I spent all my time on the bikes and the web site rather than the customers and figuring out if people really wanted it. You remember how sure we were that people would love the finished product? Well, it turns out people don't buy products!"

"They don't buy products?" She sounded confused. Had every right to be. That was Owen 36 hours ago.

"Yep! I know. It makes sense if you actually think about it. People don't buy products—they buy solutions to their problems. See? See the little difference. And I never took the time to figure out if ReBicycle was solving a real problem. Or any problem, for that matter. I just never took the time to talk to potential customers. That's what I should have started with."

Silence.

"Hello? Did I lose you again?"

"No, I'm here."

"So what do you think?"

"Well . . . I'm digesting it. I thought you were going to talk about poker and your day, and now you're saying you launched ReBicycle too soon?"

"Exactly!"

"Okay. How again?"

"We skipped the part where you really try to figure out whether it will work and went straight to the part where you start spending money. Doesn't that make sense? But it's not too late. I can still test out my assumptions and figure out what's missing. That's what I'm all excited about."

Another silence. Owen knew it wasn't the connection this time. Finally, Lisa spoke slowly, deliberately. It's how she spoke when she was choosing her words carefully.

"So are you saying that you want to start from scratch?"

"No, I just finally feel like I understand where I went wrong. And I think there might be a way to fix it. I just need to put in some time—not a year, not anything close to that—but I need to put in enough time talking to people and figuring out if there's a problem that ReBicycle could solve."

Owen could tell Lisa wasn't happy. He quickly tried to change the subject. "So you wanna hear what this one guy at my table was wearing? So get this, there's a bunch of spoons—"

"Owen!"

"Yeah?" He could tell she wasn't going to let him off the hook that fast.

"Honey, we've been at this for over a year. We've burned through a lot more money than we set aside for this business. I feel like our whole life has been on hold for the last year. I hardly ever see you, and when I do, your mind is still on ReBicycle. I thought we were going to close it down. Move on with our lives. Maybe start a family."

"I know it hasn't been easy. Not at all. I'm sorry for that. I just think you might be overreact—uh, no, what I mean to say is I think you're not understanding. I'm not talking about doing anything drastic. Just a few interviews while I'm here in Vegas. That's it. Just do some interviews and see where it goes."

"I know you say that now, but we've—"

"Look, before we get too focused on this, I haven't even told you the big news from today! You ready?"

"Sure."

"I'm now officially only half a day away from getting into the money! Knock on wood, but if I play smart and get some good cards, I could actually make back a good chunk of what ReBicycle has spent in the last year."

"Really?"

"Yes! And regardless of what happens with the business, we might at least be able to pay off some of our debt. So how's this for a deal? If I get knocked out of the tournament before I make any real money, then I'll come home and shut down ReBicycle immediately. Otherwise, I'll just keep looking into this thing while I'm here. Is that fair?"

"How many people are left in the tournament?"

"About 1,700. The top 650 are in the money."

"Seventeen hundred? You've got to knock out another 1,000 people?"

"No, I'm off tomorrow. I've made it through. After the smoke clears tomorrow, there will be something like 900 people left. Then I've just gotta survive 250 people, or stay in the top 75 percent, as I look at it."

"Well don't do anything that would put you in that 25 percent."

"I won't. I'm not. I'm playing really well."

"Knock on wood."

"Yeah, knock on wood."

The storm had passed. Somewhat calm again.

"Hey Lees, I'm going to try and go to bed. You need to get some sleep, too."

"Yeah. If you call me tomorrow, wait until the afternoon. I've got some work in the morning."

"Will do."

"Oh, and hey, Owen, one more thing. What's your new guru's name? Is he someone I would've heard of?"

"What guru?"

"The entrepreneur you met, who's giving you all this great advice. What's his name?"

"You mean Sam?"

"Yeah, I guess. Is he someone I should know?"

"Uh, I doubt it. Do you know a company called Sparksys? That was Sam's startup. It just sold for like $40 million or something."

"Wow. I hope some of that rubs off on you. That's very nice of him to be so generous with his time."

"Yeah, no kidding."

"He must be a hell of a guy."

"Uhhhhhh, not so much."

"Huh?"

"But one hell of an entrepreneur."

"Well, tell him I said thanks! Whatever he's doing is bringing you some good luck. Night."

Yeah, yeah. Owen knew. He should have told Lisa that Sam wasn't a guy but the conversation was already rocky and could have easily turned into a big fight. He'd tell Lisa eventually. After all, he hadn't technically lied. And, he assured himself, there was nothing to hide.

Chapter 15

The Secret to Customer Interviews Is Nonleading, Open-Ended Questions

S lowly. Move the arms first. Okay, they're moving pretty well. Now try the legs, left leg first. Pretty good. Right le—ooooow. Yep, Owen was still sore from the crash. He knew he would be. There had been a turning point around the age of 27 when some switch had turned off and suddenly crashes, scrapes, and bruises all hurt twice as long as they used to. That's why he'd left a bottle of ibuprofen by the bed last night. Except it wasn't by the bed. Where was it? Shit. He must have left it in the bathroom. All right, up and at 'em, kid.

He got out of bed slowly. Gingerly. On the way to the bathroom, he took his phone off the charger. He had a text from Lisa wishing him a good night. He was glad she had called him last night. He felt weird about not telling Lisa that Sam was a woman. It was just too complicated to explain, and it would take attention away from ReBicycle and the opportunity he had to test his business and figure out if there was anything in the model he needed to tweak. She didn't seem to understand, but she listened, and she tried to be supportive.

Owen turned off his alarm—it was set for 10 A.M., but no need—he was too excited to sleep. He hadn't been this excited about ReBicycle in a while. A long while. It was only 8 A.M., though, which meant play had just started and the lobby below would be a madhouse. Today was the last day of the second round. Sam would make it through today. That was for sure. Maybe he'd even visit her after he was done, let her know what he learned and get his bike back. Or would she be too focused on poker? One thing at a time. He still needed to get ready. He popped the ibuprofen. What about a shower? Didn't work out yesterday, but the stale sweat of sitting at a table too long was bothering him . . . yeah, let's try a shower.

Fortunately, the water didn't sting . . . as bad. After the shower and some coffee, and finally finding the exact shirt he needed, he was ready to go by 9 A.M. Perfect. The shirt even had a couple of wrinkles from being at the bottom of his luggage, which added some authenticity to his character.

On his way to the elevator, he took one look at the poker floor—it was still packed this early in the morning. Owen told himself he was just looking around to look around. Really, he was looking for Sam, but he couldn't admit it to himself. No luck. C'mon. Work to do.

Owen took the elevator two floors down to the hotel mall. He saw the bike shop. They were opening for the day. He noticed he was breathing faster, shallow breaths. Slow it down. Be cool. Sell it. Owen approached a too-cool-for-school kid that was installing new brakes on a beautiful old baby-blue LeMond.

"Hey, man. Is Chris here?"

"Chris. No. He's at a Crit-race right now. Can I help you?"

"Yeah. My name is Owen. I'm with Shimano Engineering—the Northwest Region." Owen pointed to his specially picked out T-shirt, which had Shimano's logo on it and which he'd gotten as free schwag from a stand at a bike show. "I called him about a survey we're doing for a new project."

"Cool, man. Chris isn't here right now. If you leave your name tho—"

"Yeah. The thing is, we're looking to get into the bike business ourselves. Instead of just building the Ultegra line of gears, we're thinking of building an Ultegra frame. You know what I'm saying?" It was Owen's best chill northern Californian accent. The kid was still eyeing him suspiciously.

"Yeah, man. That sounds cool, man. But Chris isn't here . . . I can't purchase anything without a manager."

Owen realized the issue.

"No. I think you misunderstood. I'm not with sales or marketing, dude. I'm with the R&D department. We're not selling anything yet. It's still being designed. We're asking serious bike shops if we can ask their customers about what they're looking for. I'm not selling anything." Pregnant pause. The kid was on the cusp. "And man, Chris said it was cool."

A shrug. "Hey, man, if you talked to Chris."

"Yeah. So what's your name?"

"Carter."

"Well, Carter, I'll tell you what I told Chris. I've got a list of questions here. All open-ended. We're looking for dialogue, suggestions from road bike enthusiasts."

"Cool by me."

Another pregnant pause. Carter was not the talkative type. Then again, he hadn't tried to call his manager Chris either, which Owen had been worried about. Owen looked at his watch. 9:30 A.M. It was going to be a good day.

"Carter, can I ask you a question?"

"What's up, man?" Carter plopped down in a big comfy chair near the register. Owen noticed a red and black tattoo wrapping around the front of Carter's left shin. Either a snake or some sort of flames, Owen couldn't tell.

"My name is Owen. You can call me Owen. Just wondering if you ride?"

"Course, man. Built my bike from scratch. Specialized carbon frame. Campi gears—no offense to Shimano—but I do got some Shimano pedals."

"Nice, Carter."

"I'll always take free stuff, though."

"I'll see what I can do. So what type of customer do you get in here? Are they like you? Hardcore road bikers?" Owen was leaning against the counter now, trying to look as relaxed as Carter seemed to be at his place of employment.

"Eh. Depends. A lot of Europeans with too much money. A lot of old people trying to get in shape."

Owen looked around the empty store. "And when do they start showing up?"

"Dude. I mean man. I mean Owen. We don't open until 10. I just came in early to do some tune-ups. Don't worry. We've had a lot of customers this week. The World Series of Poker is here, you know. Tons of walk-through traffic."

That's exactly what Owen wanted to hear—a large swath of potential bike riders. After grabbing a cup of coffee and a Red Bull for Carter, Owen had his clipboard out at 10 A.M. on the dot. Twenty minutes later, the bike shop—L'Alpe Cyclery—had its first customer. It was an older gentleman with a young woman in yoga pants. Owen waited for Carter to approach them, but apparently this bike shop preferred the indirect approach. After letting them peruse a line of mid-range Trek frames, Owen finally approached them. He made the sure the clipboard was visible. His palms were noticeably sweaty. This was scarier than he thought it would be.

"Hi there. My name is Owen from Shimano. I was hoping to ask you a few questions for a new produc—"

"Sorry." The man put up his hand and walked past Owen without making eye contact. Reengage? No. It didn't seem right. But the couple was still in the store! Finally, after five minutes, they left. If Carter had noticed them, he hadn't let on.

Another customer entered the store. Just by eyeing him, Owen took him for somebody who was in the WSOP and had the day off like him. Again, no approach by Carter. Owen decided to try a different tactic.

"Hey. How you doing in the tournament?"

"Excuse me?"

"You in the World Series?"

"Yeah."

"So you going strong? Almost in the money, right?" The guy gave Owen a curious stare. At least he hadn't said no yet.

"Yeah. It's the last day of the second round. I played the second round yesterday. Got today off."

"Cool, man." If this small talk is what it took from Owen, then so be it.

"I'm just looking around. . . ."

"Oh, no worries man." Wow, was he already starting to sound like Carter? "I actually don't work here. I work for Shimano." Point to the shirt. "You know, the gear folks?"

"Yeah. I ride Shimano."

"Thanks. I'm glad to hear that. I'm actually here for the tournament myself. Just meeting and greeting, you know? My name is Owen, by the way."

"Dan."

"Dan. Nice to meet you." Go for the kill! Owen glanced down at his legs. They were small. No matter, he was here and Owen had his attention. "You ride a fair amount, don't you, Dan?"

A blush.

"Well . . . not as much as I should."

A conspiratorial look by Owen. He'd practiced it. "Hey, Dan. You know . . . well, I shouldn't tell you this. It's still in development. But we at Shimano, we're coming out with our own bike. Planning to. Frame and everything."

"Really?"

Owen couldn't tell if he meant it or was just trying to be polite. Keep plowing on.

"So let me ask you, Dan. I mean we're still in the R&D phase, but that's where I work. That's what I'm trying to figure out. How to sell this thing."

"Okay."

"So you already own a road bike?"

"Well, my brother-in-law gave me his old one. A year ago or so. It's been good, but you know, I've thought about upgrading. I've been looking online."

Owen couldn't contain his excitement! Dan was the perfect ReBicycle customer.

"Oh, so you've been shopping online for bikes?"

"No."

"No?" Now Owen was confused.

"I've been looking at the manufacturers' pages online. Trek. Specialized. Cilo. Then, there's a bike shop by my house where they have these demos, and so I've tested a couple out. And I'm thinking if I do well tomorrow, why not? You know?"

"Oh." Don't show your disappointment, Owen! "You mind if I ask you a couple of questions. I mean, you're the type of customer we'd really like to have with Shimano."

The small talk had put Dan at ease. "Sure."

"So Dan. We're considering a lot of different factors right now. I mean price, manufacturing quality, frame material, weight, components, design options, you name it. Are there any factors that would affect your decision more than others?"

"Out of those? What were they again?"

"Hold on a sec. I've got a clipboard. This is informal. I actually brought this for him." Owen pointed to Carter, who was doing something on his phone and oblivious. "But I'd like your opinion as well, Dan. All right. We got price, quality, frame material, weight, components, design options, brand, gear components."

Dan took a look at the list Owen had printed off in the business center of the hotel less than an hour before. "All of those."

"Any of them more than others?"

"Quality. First and foremost."

"Any of them less important than others?"

"What were the options again?" Dan took another look at the sheet. "I don't really consider design options—you mean like colors, right? I don't care about that."

Dan hadn't brought it up, but Owen had to ask. He had to! How many people were going to be as receptive as Dan? "And would you say that the prices of bikes at stores like this one are low, high, or about right?"

"It seems like prices are about the same wherever you go . . . you get what you pay for. On Trek and Giant's web site, there's a suggested retail price, so I know what my bike shop is charging me."

"Okay, and on a scale of 1 to 10, how big a problem is price?"

"Price? Maybe a 2."

"A 2?"

"They're all the same. I mean specialized carbon frames cost about the same as any others."

"Right. So price is a 2?" Owen still couldn't believe it.

"I was shocked by prices when I first started riding, but they're the same all over. I bought my son a Huffy not long ago for Christmas and couldn't believe how cheap it was. But it's also already rusting. You get what you pay for."

"What about Craigslist or eBay?"

"I'm not buying a bike on eBay. Even cheap bikes are $700. I know that's not a lot of money to a lot of people here, but I run a small business and have three kids and a wife—$700 is a lot of textbooks. If I spend that much on a bike and it turns out to be worthless, then my wife is never going to let me buy another one, and if I come home from Vegas with a bike, my wife is not going to care whether it cost $700 or two grand. It's still a bike we don't need. So why not spend the extra dough on something I know."

Even Owen had to admit Dan had a point. Time to cut through the crap. "Dan, is there any way you'd buy a bike online?"

Dan looked to be considering the question, but only for a brief moment. "Not one I hadn't ridden. Sorry if you or Shimano is trying to go the Internet route, but I need to test a bike. It's more personal than a car, you know?"

"Oh, I know."

"Well, then. Any more questions?" Dan seriously looked like he wanted to answer more questions, but Owen had none.

"Nope."

"Good luck. Shimano bikes! They should be good!" He pumped his fist.

Dan left the store. Again, Carter had not made a move to try to make a sale.

Chapter 16

The Only Way to Get Good at Customer Interviews Is to Practice

"Ladies and gentlemen, welcome to the second round of the World Series of Poker! Congratulations on being one of the top 2,700 poker players in the world. Today, only the top 450 players will advance to the next round. Joining us this morning to open play is honorary pit boss and former Nevada governor . . ."

Sam looked at the table. Nobody was paying attention to the emcee. They were all too busy stacking chips or preparing their small portion of the table to their exact liking—warriors preparing for battle in their own way. Sam was pleased to see her stack was among the biggest, maybe the biggest at the table. She looked around the room. She tried to make out some pros she might know.

Phil Helmuth was still in it. Her thoughts were interrupted by the only words that mattered:

"Good luck, players! Shuffle up and deal!"

And with that, the second day was off. As she stacked and restacked her chips, Sam considered her goal—obviously, the big target was to make it to the end of the day. That was totally doable. Especially with her stack. She just needed to control herself through early play.

That was easier said than done. This was supposed to be the pros! Almost 5,000 players had already gone home. Yet everybody seemed to be just as worried as Sam about getting to the third day. Maybe it was just her table, but no one seemed to be chasing any pots. It didn't even help when Sam hit an incredible streak of cards—pocket aces and a pocket pair of kings in an hour. Pocket queens. Jack-queen suited. Ace-queen suited. It seemed as if she had a high face card every hand. And to show for this amazing run? A total net of 10 grand or so. Nobody would chase! Nobody would play! It was driving her mad.

It was also getting tough to focus. Because so few hands were being played, there were long stretches of time where she could literally zone out and not miss a thing. And then, all of a sudden, there'd be somebody in the small blind coming in for a big bet and it'd already be her turn and she'd have to decide immediately. It went like that three or four times—complete boredom followed by several seconds of pee-your-pants excitement. This must be what it's like to be a goalkeeper in soccer or a firefighter or something. Sam couldn't decide. She couldn't think. She didn't like this style of play. She wasn't used to it. It was totally different than her first day. It might as well have been a completely different game altogether.

She was getting frustrated. Nobody would play. It was like everyone at this table was in ultra-conservative mode and she hated it. It also gave her plenty of time to think about nonpoker stuff, which was exactly what she didn't want. For some reason, she was obsessed with getting that bike out of the back of her car. As soon as the day was done, she'd call Owen and tell him to get it. He was the reason she was feeling down. She was almost sure of that. What with all his moping.

And now, he was becoming a little too friendly, coming up to her hotel room. Asking her for favors. Yes, it was probably best to make a clean break. But before she could do that, she had to get rid of that damn bike. She wondered if Owen was really doing customer interviews today. She thought back to how hard it was to learn. How to ask nonleading questions. How to pry for further information. How to recognize those dilated pupils when there was something there.

She thought back to her first customer interviews and how hard it was to not try and sell them something during the initial conversation, but really find out what they were thinking. It was amazing how people wanted to be nice and would just lie right to your face if they thought you were looking for a particular response. You almost had to trick them into revealing what they really thought.

Sam remembered lecturing her employees on getting the most out of these interviews. **Don't use 'would you'! Those are the worst two words you can start a sentence with! Don't ask yes or no questions. Make sure you are giving them plenty of opportunities to tell their story. Their true feelings aren't going to be the direct answers to your questions, but in the stories they tell you around their answers. We don't care about anything they have to say about the future. Only how they act and feel in the present and the past.**

She missed it.

Sam shook her head and focused. Play was coming back around to her. She needed to focus on cards. She didn't need to think about the bike in the back of her car. Or Owen. Or anything.

Focus on the cards, Sam.

Chapter 17

Finding Out Your Assumptions Were Wrong Is Just as Valuable as Proving Them Right

By mid-afternoon, Owen had enough. Twenty-seven interviews. Twenty-seven! Not one person had listed price above a five. Were these people crazy? What did Las Vegas do to your internal compass that people in America did not care about price? After all, this was the land of dollar stores and dollar menus. Granted, the overlapping Venn diagram of people who bought composite carbon bike frames and shopped daily at Dollar Stores was probably small, but it existed. It had to exist. This was America, dammit!

Owen had even avoided the internationals who came into the store. Among the American crowd, there had been a couple of "can't talk right now" folks, but really those 27 interviews represented a good half of the people that had entered the store. They'd all mentioned quality being high on their list. One guy said he comparison-shopped online, and then there was that couple that was considering a used bike. But even they had mentioned quality! How was it possible that none of the 27 people he talked to listed price as their number one issue?

When Owen had asked similar questions over a year ago, he thought he remembered a bunch of people telling him price was an overwhelming issue. Did he lead them to say that? Were they just confirming his own bias? No. There had to be other people out there. Maybe he was talking to the wrong customer segment, as Sam would say. The wrong group of people who would make good customers for his business.

He had to find those right people. Owen took a look at Carter. He might be the worst salesman Owen has ever met. His only sale had been because a man had literally shouted at Carter until he took out his ear-buds and asked him if they still had that bike he'd ridden a while ago. That was one of the people who'd blown Owen off. That guy was not the type Owen was targeting. Too old. Too thin. Too everything. He was wearing freaking Arc'teryx in Las Vegas! Ugh. Casinos had a way of distorting reality. Get back to reality, Owen.

Owen looked at his phone. 3 P.M. Enough. He bid Carter a quick goodbye and got a thumbs-up and a "yeah, man" in return. It was definitely this bike store that was the problem. Two floors up on the elevator and it seemed like a different world. It was a familiar world—after all, Owen would be playing in this world tomorrow. The crowd had thinned since he'd last been here at 9 this morning. Still a lot of players left, though. He actively searched the crowd for Sam. Surprisingly, spotting a blonde female was harder than he'd expected. A good five minutes of scanning got him no results. Time for plan B.

Owen started walking the spectator galleys surrounding the tables. He hadn't thought they'd be crowded, but again, he was wrong. These rounds weren't even televised, so why were people already here watching it? A quick thought about how tomorrow there'd be even bigger crowds watching him play. No. Don't think about that. Find Sam.

Ten minutes later, he still hadn't found her. Is it possible? Was Sam already out of the tournament? Owen got out his phone to text her and then decided against it. No—losing in the tournament was worth a phone call. But the galleys forbid phone calls—only texts allowed—so Owen had to make his way to the foyer again, and there she was. Literally at the first table.

"Sam!" He shouted.

She turned around. "Oh, hey, Owen." She seemed surprised. He was excited to see her. It was weird. Nothing but bad news for five hours, and yet that was all washed away by finding Sam.

Don't forget about the bike, Owen.

"Hey, Sam. How you doing?" It was a stupid question. You could tell how somebody was doing by their chip count, and hers was massive.

"Good. How are you doing?"

"I need to borrow your keys. I want to return my bike."

"Now?"

"Yeah. Why? Do you need the SUV for a pedicure appointment or something? I feel like you're going to be tied up here for a few more hours."

"No. Hold on." Sam waited for another hand to be dealt and quickly folded. She got up from the table and went over to Owen. She looked alluring making her way to the galley. Must be all that extra oxygen they are pumping in here. Finally, she was close enough they could talk in a normal voice.

"What's up?"

"Listen. It's a long story, but I've been doing a lot of interviews. Like what you said. Not exactly what you said, but I took some things to heart and . . ."

"And?"

"I need to borrow your keys. I need to go back to the bike store."

"Okay. No worries. What's happening with the interviews, though?"

"I don't think I've been able to talk to any normal people yet. I think it's a casino, Las Vegasy thing. That's why I want to go to this bike shop. I know there's locals there. Not casino, World Series folk."

"So it's not been good news, then?"

"The keys, Sam."

She went back to the table and got them out of her backpack. She was handing them to Owen when she pulled them back.

"Hey, I'm giving these to you on one condition." She was looking at him the way a teacher looks at a student performing below his potential.

"What?"

"You tell me what you find out."

"Okay."

"I'm serious. Don't just okay me. Let me know. I'm interested."

"Okay."

"Promise me, Owen!" She added a cutesy grin and dangled the keys higher in the air.

"I said okay, Sam. I promise."

"Roof of the parking garage. Don't use all my gas, Mister." She poked him in the chest. "And I made you promise because I don't think you're hearing what you thought you were going to hear."

Owen turned to leave and shouted, "We'll see about that!" over his shoulder.

He had the routine from this morning down cold. How to approach people. How to get their attention. How to frame the questions. Finally, he'd get some real people who cared about real things like price. Owen knew it—he'd been that real person. First things first, though—see the damage to the bike in the daylight and try to find the bike store.

The first task proved easy—Owen's body had taken the majority of the impact, and besides some scratches on the handlebars and some sand and dirt that needed to be cleaned off, the bike was good to go. The bike store proved more elusive. Owen estimated the taxi from the hotel had taken 15 minutes. Tops. Yet it took almost an hour to get there—damn the traffic.

When Owen walked in, he was relieved to see it wasn't the same gangly teenager who had rented him his bike. This guy was a little older, a little more mature. He said "hey" when Owen entered. Owen already liked him better than Carter.

"What happened to you?"

"Had to lay the bike down. Car came out of nowhere." A little white lie to gain sympathy wouldn't hurt anyone.

"Oh, that blows. Unfortunately, it happens more often than you would think."

"I'm just happy it wasn't any more serious than it was. I'm Owen."

"Jeff. Any other issues with the bike?" Jeff was starting to check boxes on a little form.

"No . . . didn't get to ride it as much as I'd like because of the accident but it was nice for what it is. I hadn't ridden anything this heavy since those old Raleigh frames."

That got a laugh from Jeff.

"You know, we still have some of those. They're indestructible. People bring them in to get worked on all the time . . . you ride a lot?"

Here was the opening.

"Actually, I'm in the biz. I have a store back east." No need to say it's an online store. "And I was wondering, Jeff, if I could ask a favor."

Jeff checked the final box at the bottom of the form. "Sure."

"My store isn't doing so hot. Tough economy and all, but that still doesn't explain it. I think I need to talk to some people who are buying bikes elsewhere. Get a feel for what they're looking for.

"Okay."

"And I was wondering if I could do it here. I mean I'm already here. It's my only off-day from the World Series of Poker—I lucked into a ticket—and I can't do it in my hometown. I'm not selling anything. I'm not pressuring anyone. I just want to ask some people who come in some general questions. I know it's an unusual request, but what do you say?"

"Uh . . ."

"I promise I'll be out of here by sundown."

"Well . . ."

"And I'll give you a hundred bucks for the inconvenience."

"$150."

Jeff was a better businessman than Owen had given him credit for.

"Deal. But in that case, you gotta help me. Just introduce me to people you know who are picking up bikes for repair and that sort of stuff."

"Deal."

It didn't take long before the first customer came in. But in the meantime, Owen learned a little about Jeff. He was a former swimmer who had come close to making the Olympic team. He moved to Vegas to follow his girlfriend. He was the manager and had hopes of buying the store from the current owner. More importantly, Jeff also considered price important.

Unfortunately, Jeff did not buy bikes anymore, but rather put them together from parts of bikes people never picked up. It was sort of like ReBicycle's business model but on a micro-scale. Owen even threw out the ReBicycle name casually in conversation to see the reaction on Jeff's face, but if he had heard of ReBicycle before, he didn't show it. That was not a good sign. Finally, a couple came in to pick up a bike they had preordered for their son. They weren't ideal subjects, but at this point in the day, Owen would take whatever he could get.

"Hey, folks. How you doing?"

"Fine." The wife took control. Curt but friendly.

"Hey. I couldn't help but overhear that you're buying a road bike for your son."

"Yes."

"I'm just curious but what made you decide on this bike?" He pointed at the Trek that Jeff was applying some grease to.

"Our son wanted it."

"And how old is your son?"

"Thirteen. Excuse me . . . who are you?"

"I run a bike shop back in Ohio. I'm in town for the tournament. Just curious."

"Well, he wanted this bike. He helps around the house and it's good exercise, so that's what we got him."

"That's an awfully expensive bike for a 13-year-old."

"That's what I thought, but that's what all the bikes cost. He's talking about racing and you can't race or be serious on something cheap."

"You really think so?"

"I know so. We looked around. Went to REI and several bike stores."

"What about online? That's where everything is these days, it seems."

"No. We tried at first, but the prices weren't that different to justify buying sight unseen."

"Yeah. But you can pick up used bikes pretty cheap."

She laughed and pointed to Jeff.

"He told us not to bother. That all physical bike stores carry used bikes. Sure, we looked at several around town, but the difference between getting a new one that our son could customize versus one where who knows what was done with it, well, it wasn't worth it."

Owen tried to hide his shock. "Jeff, you didn't say anything about selling used bikes." Jeff looked surprised, either by Owen's accusatory tone or by the fact that he was randomly brought back into the conversation.

"Are you kidding? Every bike shop sells used bikes. Mainly trade-ins. We keep them on this rack." Jeff pointed to a row right behind Owen. Sure enough, Owen hadn't even noticed that the bikes right behind him were used. They were all good-looking—obviously cleaned up—but now looking closely, he could see scratches and scuffs here and there, and even some well-worn tires.

"Does every bike shop in town sell used bikes?"

"You're telling me your shop doesn't?"

"Uh . . . no. We've thought about it, but no."

"Maybe that's your problem right there."

Owen was replaying every bike shop he ever visited before ReBicycle in his head. Did they all sell used bikes? There was Astra Bikes—they had used bikes, yeah, but only a couple. New England Bike definitely did not . . . well, except occasionally the one or two they'd display. Several other stores he couldn't remember for sure either one way or the other.

"Shit!"

Jeff and the couple gave Owen a puzzled look. Guess that was aloud.

"I'm sorry."

Jeff was still eyeing him. "You okay?"

"Yeah." To the couple. "Thank you for your time. Your son is very lucky to have this bike."

"Uh. Thanks."

After the couple left, it was back to just Jeff and Owen. A heavy minute passed, and Owen knew it was up to him to break the ice.

"Hey, Jeff, I'm sorry."

"Look. I don't know what kind of bike store you're running back east, but normally we try not to swear at customers here."

"I was . . . I was zoning out. Information overload, you know. I just can't believe a couple like that would spend that much money on a bike."

"Yeah. We get a lot of sticker shock at first here. I'm sure you do, as well. But that's mainly from people who don't know what they're getting into. Like you've probably noticed the surge around the Tour de France. People see it on television and think the bikes look cool and can help them get in shape, and then they realize, whoa!"

Owen was interested, "So what happens to those customers?"

"Same thing that happens at your store probably. You can spot them a mile away. Ninety percent of them come in once or twice and you never see them again. The other 10 percent rent a demo, and then maybe one or two of those actually buy a bike and fall for the sport."

"Just out of curiosity—how many of your customers would you say demo bikes before buying?

"Here? Everyone. You're stupid if you don't. That's why people buy in person still. You can't get the feel of a bike online and even if one day you could, are you going to mail it back every time you want a tune-up? That's why I think there's value in taking over this store, because I know bike shops are going to be around as long as people need tune-ups and repairs."

A ringing. The door had opened. A wiry, thin man in his early 40s entered the shop.

Owen swallowed hard. No cursing. He looked at his watch and told himself three more hours of interviews.

Chapter 18

Don't Pivot to a New Idea without Testing Your New Assumptions

There are times when a phone call is more than a phone call. When it needs to be picked up. When it's like a life preserver thrown into the water and demands a response. Now was one of those times. 9 P.M. was what Columbus time? Midnight? That's not too late!

"Hi. You've reached Lisa. If you leave your name—" Click. Lying on the bed in his room, Owen had stripped down to his boxers and an undershirt. He laid the phone on his chest and stared at the ceiling.

So Lisa didn't pick up. No big deal. She'd call back. Tonight or very first thing tomorrow. He just needed to talk to her after the day he had. His phone rang, and he held it up in the air between his eyes and his view of the ceiling. It showed an unknown number. Must be Lisa calling from the fax line or something. He answered it while sitting up.

"Hey, babe!"

"Well hello to you, too, sweet cheeks."

"Oh, hey, Sam."

"You've still got my car keys."

"Shit. Yeah. They're in my pants. Do you need them right now?"

"No, but I'll need them soon. Did you return your bike?"

"Yeah. After I found the place."

"You do anything else today?"

"Ten hours of interviews."

"Yeah? What did you learn?"

A buzz. Lisa was on the other line.

"Sam. I got the missus calling."

"Got it. My keys."

"Okay. Hey—real quick, you made it through today, right?"

"Is Paris the capital of France?"

"Good. I'll see you tomorrow, then, before the third round begins."

Owen pressed over. He changed his voice to slightly sleepy.

"Did I wake you, Owen?"

"No, babe. How you doing?"

"What a week at work! Margaret called in sick for like the tenth time this quarter, so guess who had to cover her class. Me. And it was her ESL class today, so the kids don't speak English and I don't speak Spanish and it was a disaster . . . and I miss you. You said you'd be home by now."

"I said there was the possibility I would be. But I'm still in the tournament."

"Are you making money yet? Does that question make sense?"

"Yeah. But no. I mean yeah, it makes sense that I should be in the money by now, but the first two rounds take five days to complete because there are so many players. Tomorrow is the third round, and if I make it through tomorrow, then we make money."

"Oh." She sounded bored, yet slightly curious.

"It's like I was telling you yesterday, I had the whole day off from the tournament today. So I decided to spend the day at a couple of bike shops doing interviews."

"Right, for your friend Sam or someone."

"Well, not for Sam, but thanks to Sam's advice."

"So what did you learn?"

"Well, I've been rethinking the business."

"Rethinking ReBicycle? Have you checked the sales figures from yesterday?"

"No. Should I?" Maybe business was picking up.

"Not really."

"That was the answer I was afraid of. Do you have a minute? I know it's late there, but let me run an idea by you."

"Okay, but not too long. It's past midnight already, and I may have to teach that ESL class again tomorrow."

Owen knew she wanted to talk about her job. He knew that it was best to let her. Whatever helps her get over work. Just get the bombshell out of the way and see how she reacts.

"Okay, babe. Just hear me out. What would you think about a physical store?"

"Huh?"

"A physical store. A physical ReBicycle. Instead of trying to capture an online audience, we go the other direction. We take it local. We try to get people in the area. I mean, I'm just throwing it out there, and we'd keep the web site, of course, but instead get a location and be, you know, like more normal." He'd done his part. He'd thrown it out there.

"Why would we do that?"

"Because ReBicycle is not working! It's just not working, honey! And it's eating me up. The fact that you can't quit your job. The fact that I'm not asking how many bikes we sold. If we had a physical store, we could focus on maintenance. You could work in the store. It may be better. Sam told me to reconsider all of my assumptions, and I'm thinking that the biggest mistake I made was not seeing what was right in front of me. In front of us! And that's a lot of local people who need freaking bikes and need their bikes worked on."

Owen had hit on this plan while driving back from the second bike shop. After speaking to nearly 40 potential customers, he had heard a pretty resounding message. Price didn't matter nearly as much as he thought—not even close—and even worse than that, people didn't want to buy bicycles online.

The long drive back gave Owen plenty of time to figure out how he had made such a huge oversight in his business. It was something Sam had said about truly investigating people's opinions rather than trying to sell them. That was his mistake at the beginning. When he first got started, he didn't talk to many people he didn't already know, and when he asked them about ReBicycle, he would steer them into an answer virtually no one would say no to: "If you could buy a bike with the quality of a brand new Trek bike at almost half the price, would you be interested?" What a stupid question! Owen could clearly see it now. He never even thought to ask anything about people buying them online.

"So . . . you want to start over? How can we afford to do that?"

Now *that* was a great question. They were financially on tilt already. Owen wasn't even sure Lisa knew to what extent. But he could figure it out. Owen was sure of that. First, he needed Lisa on board with this idea of a physical store; everything else would follow. The store seemed like his only lifeline out of this mess, the only thing that would save him from true defeat and failure, and Owen was willing to do anything to avoid that fate.

"No, it's not starting over at all. I'm thinking of combining ReBicycle into a physical store. We'd figure out the money. There are a lot of rich people here. Sam is an investor. Sam might be interested. That's just one option. There are all kinds of options."

It was hard wiggling through that sentence about Sam without the use of any pronouns, but he wanted to let Lisa know that there were money options out there.

"Owen, honey, it's after midnight here."

"What? You don't like it?" Owen stood up and started pacing around in his room.

"It's after midnight. I have to work in the morning. Can we talk about it tomorrow?"

"Babe, I've had such a long day of hearing person after person tell me what an idiot I was for launching ReBicycle the way I did. It would just mean a lot to me if you said we could try this one other option. I just need to know what you think."

"I think . . . well, I think you're right. We need to do something."

"Okay." That sounded like a positive sign.

"And it sounds like what you've figured out is that we started spending money getting ReBicycle up and running before we were ready. That we should have talked to more people initially."

"Yeah. That's totally what I did."

"Well . . . it sounds like you may be doing that again. Wanting to jump into something else without getting feedback from enough other people."

"But that's all I did all day, honey. I watched people come into bike shops to buy and fix their bikes. I'm not reinventing the wheel here."

"Look, Owen, I think that maybe ReBicycle may be like my friend Ann's jewelry business. You know, she makes good money with her jewelry parties."

Uh . . . that came out of left field.

"I'm not following."

"Well, Ann makes money with jewelry. But it's extra money. She has a job at that bank—First Financial or whatever it's called. And then she sells jewelry on the side. Why couldn't we just downsize ReBicycle?"

"And I do what exactly on the side?"

"Well, you'll figure it out."

Now it was Owen's turn not to argue. He knew Lisa was referring to going back to consulting. To his old firm. But just two years ago he and Lisa had started marriage counseling and her number one issue with him had been work. He did too much of it with consulting and he did not enjoy it, and she could feel that seeping into the house. The same way he could now feel her unhappiness in the admin job at the school seeping into all aspects of her life. How could she possibly allude to his going back? It was almost blasphemous! Once he quit, it was like folding a hand. And once you fold, you can't unfold. How could she imply that he should unfold? Okay. Enough. Don't get mad.

"Hey, babe. I know it's late. You're right, we should talk about this more tomorrow. I've gotta get up and play. And you've got school."

"It's not just the money I'm worried about. I . . . it would just be hard to watch you start another thing from scratch. I'm just tired of delaying our lives for this thing. Delaying seeing you on a regular basis. Delaying any vacations or just getting away together. Delaying . . . all kinds of things."

Owen rubbed his furrowed brow and sat back down on the bed. He now understood that Lisa was worried about another year of startup life. She had every right to be; it had been a very difficult year.

"I don't want to delay any of those things, honey. I just . . . I just don't want to fail. I don't want to fail as a business owner, as a husband and provider, as a father robbing his future kids of financial security. I just need this to work."

She didn't respond. Was that a quiet sobbing on the other end of the line?

"Are you crying, babe?"

"No," she said, followed by a sniffle.

Ughh. Why do so many of their ReBicycle conversations lead to this?

"Owen, I just don't think I can handle another year of this. Another six months. I feel like we are just business partners, and I want to be your wife and the mother of your kids, and every time you figure out a way to try one more thing, I just feel that idea slipping farther and farther away."

"I'm sorry, honey. I shouldn't have brought this up over the phone. Let's give this a few days to breathe and then talk about it after I get home, okay?"

More sniffles. "Okay."

She was a good wife. Owen was lucky to have someone who would endure the past year and be open to doing it all over again. That's dedication. For some reason Owen's mind went to three weeks ago when he got food poisoning right after a meal at a Mexican place (a place he'd insisted they eat even though she wanted pizza) and what did she do? She changed the sheets three times after he threw up on them. She went to the store to get stomach medicines and brought back movies that they watched together. She'd slept next to him that night even when he wouldn't have slept next to himself, if he could have helped it. Sometimes, it takes moments like that to realize how lucky you are.

"So, babe, what happens if Margaret doesn't show tomorrow?"

"Well . . ." She was back in a conversational tone. "Patrice was saying that Margaret had used so many sick days that she's at risk for a letter of concern in her teacher's file, which can affect . . ." Owen was feeling sleepy. But he knew this was one of the most important interviews he'd conduct all day.

Chapter 19

Save Your Chips for When You'll Need the Least Amount of Luck to Win

Poker felt so refreshing. Yeah, Owen's body still ached from the fall. Yeah, his chip stack was getting incrementally smaller. Yeah, his brain was fried from having played 20 hours of poker in the past 48 hours. But this was such a different world than business. And he was still in!

Right now his strategy consisted of a lot of folding and making conversation around the table. He liked the current table. Everybody seemed to be like him—happy to be here. Not overly competitive.

At least not until they got to the money. Owen had never thought in a thousand years he'd actually get to the money, but here he was.

The day started with only 900 players, just a fraction of the 7,200 that started round one. The top 650 were all guaranteed a cash payout of at least $20,000. Owen had seen a lot of players around other tables leave. And simple math said that having already played three hours and change, they must be getting close to that magic 650.

The other players could feel it, too. There was Tony from San Diego, who owned his own business manufacturing ultra-quality label makers for chemical companies or something like that. There was Tony 2, the Navy vet who had retired to Vegas. There was Kerry the former lawyer and currently rich wife. They were all talkative, especially Tony 2. He had asked Owen where he got all those scratches and bruises and, without really waiting for an answer, guessed a motorcycle accident, just so he could start talking about his own motorcycle accident. And then motorcycle accident number two. And then accident three on a Tokyo highway. And accident four, which had involved a bottle of Jack, a dare, an airport runway, and what was apparently the biggest-known secret on whatever fort or post he'd been serving on.

Tony 2 kept the commentary going and every one else joined in. They all seemed to want to do anything but play poker. It was like it was their table against everyone else to make it to the money. Owen had never experienced that kind of camaraderie at a poker table and was really enjoying it.

Tony 2 was now sharing about his travels to Beirut and God knows where else. Owen kept laughing, but was really starting to wish he'd paid attention to what time they'd started—how much time had gone by? They've got to be getting close. He looked around the table. He could tell people were starting to become anxious. Even Kerry, the chip leader at their table who couldn't be knocked out by any one hand, was fidgeting when bets came to her. This definitely wasn't the table you see on television! Another half-hour went by . . .

"Ladies and gentlemen, there are 655 players remaining. We will now play one hand at a time. Dealers, do not deal hands before you are authorized to do so . . ."

So they were finally there! Five players to be eliminated before Owen had a guaranteed $20,000. Well, $10,000 after he gives Pitchford his half. Owen was doing everything he could to push out of his brain all the reasons why he needed that money. That morning, Owen had decided to treat the tournament as separate from his own financial concerns, partially because he didn't want it to hinder his play and partially because he wanted more than a temporary fix for ReBicycle. A little cash infusion to continue a flawed business model was not a good strategy. He would never have admitted that just two days ago, but he fully embraced it now.

Tony 2 was the first to ask the dealer what exactly was going on. The dealer explained that all the tables would play one hand at a time, meaning all the tables would wait for the last table to finish a hand before starting the next one. That would allow the tournament officials to know exactly who went out at what number. It also meant that each hand took about 15 minutes to play, even if everybody at Owen's table folded. They would do this until they got to 650 players.

"And yours truly is no Bubble Boy!" Tony 2 quickly added. The player who went out right before the money bubble burst would be forever branded the infamous "Bubble Boy" and kick themselves for the rest of their lives for coming so close.

Owen didn't want to be the Bubble Boy either. He did some quick math; there were four hands to go before he was in the big blind, and then there would be eight hands after that he could safely fold without giving up any blinds. After he paid his big blind, he could just walk away from the table to make sure he wasn't even tempted to play or do anything stupid. It was the best way for him to save himself from getting into any trouble.

When Owen was in the small blind, the emcee came back on, "654 players left. A round of applause for Mr. Dijeep Fa . . ." So he was four from the money. Owen still couldn't believe it. It would be pretty soon before they were down to 650, but it took 20 excruciating minutes to get through his small blind hand.

Finally! He was in the big blind. Owen looked down at his hand and his heart stopped.

Pocket kings.

"You know ESPN is doing a documentary on bubble players . . ." Tony 2 was still talking as always. Owen tried to appear interested but he couldn't—call this hand? Raise it? He counted his chips, which was a dead giveaway because he had made it a point not to count them over the past two hours . . . 60 grand and change, not counting the 3 grand in the pot for the big blind. Kerry called. She was in a position of strength; Owen didn't mind taking some money off her.

Whatever it was about Kerry's call, though, the quiet guy next to her with glasses seemed to lose it. Owen couldn't remember his name, but he had maybe $20,000 in chips left, the lowest amount at the table. Owen was trying to figure out what this guy was doing and when was the last hand he'd played. Suddenly, and with force, quiet glasses pushed all of his chips toward the middle and announced, "all-in!"

Owen suddenly felt sweat everywhere. Maybe that was an exaggeration, but there were definitely beads of sweat on his leg—the road rash was burning from it. So what did quiet glasses have? Owen looked again at his pocket kings. There was exactly one starting hand better than his. Did nerd alert have pocket aces? Even if he didn't have pocket aces, Owen could still lose after all the cards were dealt. Oh, well, at least if it's between the two of them, his losses will be minimized to 20K.

Owen could hear Pitchford in his ear. "Save your chips for when you'll need the least luck to win." If there was ever a hand where Owen could minimize his potential for losses and still have a great chance to win some chips, this was it. It shouldn't matter that he was so close to the money. This was one of the best shots he would have all day.

"Call."

Everybody else cleared out of the hand, leaving just Owen and glasses. Owen flipped over his pocket kings and waited and waited.

After what felt like five minutes later, glasses flipped over 6-jack unsuited. It had been a bluff. A total gutsy move. It was a stupid move, but Owen had to give him credit for having the guts to risk doubling his entry fee just to steal some blinds when everyone was skittish. Now Owen just had to hope his luck didn't change.

The flop came down: 2, 10, jack. Owen was still in the lead, but glasses had made a pair of jacks. One more jack and Owen knew there was no way he'd make it through the end of the day. The turn card was a 5. Finally, the river. The dealer turned it over slowly as if trying to drag out the action as long as possible.

Another 10! Owen had won the pot!

He finally learned his opponent's name when the emcee weighed in. "653 players left. Let's have a round of applause for Mr. Simon Fairfax!" Owen applauded his efforts. Vaya con dios, Simon.

Owen's stack was now near 100 grand. He was out of the blinds for eight hands. Time to walk away from the table. Maybe go get a drink. No reason to get invested in a hand and do something stupid right before getting in the money. He figured it was the surest way to keep from messing this up.

Poker sure is fun when you don't have to pray for luck or inter-vention from a higher power. Owen wondered if ReBicycle could be this much fun if he spent the time testing his assumptions and relying less on hope and luck to sell bikes. Maybe he should follow Pitchford's advice in business and save his chips until he needed the least luck to win. Was opening a physical store another big gamble?

He'd have time to work on reducing his business risk later. Just enjoy this moment. You're so close to the money, Owen. You're about to be part of a very elite group of poker players.

As he walked away from the table, Owen could feel the adrena-line pumping through his body. He was just stepping off the poker floor when he heard the emcee announce, "And in 653rd place, Ms. Samantha Donovan."

What the . . .? Owen scanned the crowd but couldn't see any exceptional movement. Had he ever learned Sam's last name?

Chapter 20

Successful Entrepreneurs Recognize Failure, Fold, and Live to Fight Another Day

There were shots in front of them. Why were there shots in front of them again? They seemed familiar. Sam finally remembered. Oh yes, she'd ordered them. That was like 15 minutes ago, though. Those shots took forever to come. And they were slightly warm. Who cares? Southern Comfort and lime—her favorite. She needed some comfort. A bubble girl! Might as well write that on her tombstone—entrepreneur, investor, activist, and amateur poker player who almost made it to the money before getting knocked out just a few hands short. Whatever. Shots will help.

"Owen, take your shot."

"Okay." He didn't move.

"Stop being a pansy and take your shot."

"Sam, you're drunk."

"*You're* drunk, Oowwwwen!" Sam laughed at her witty retort. She wasn't really drunk. At least she didn't feel it. Instead, she felt liberated. Well, part of the time she felt liberated. The other part of the time she was wondering how she could have missed that flush draw. How?! How?! How?! It had been like that for the last several hours—one moment of feeling glad she didn't have the pressure of playing anymore. The next moment realizing that she should still be playing. Back and forth. Well, if Owen thought she was drunk, she might as well actually get there—it'd be the only way she'd get to sleep tonight. Again, though! How did she miss it?!

"How did I miss it?!"

"Sam, you've got to stop beating yourself up."

"I mean, it's one thing if I had called the all-in, but to initiate it and lose—on a hand where I was already beat!"

"Sam, stop it. You got unlucky. Trust me, nobody cares that you went out right before the bubble. All you gotta tell them is I missed the bubble."

"Yeah. Whatever. Easy for you to say. I hate clubs."

"I'd hardly call this bar a club."

"No. I mean I hate the suit of clubs. I hate it. I've never had a club-flush this entire tournament. I can't remember one hand where I was like, 'Man, I'm glad clubs came down.' I wasn't even looking at that club on the turn. I didn't even notice it was a club. If I had, you know what? I still would have called all-in because who the hell plays a club draw through a raise before the flop and a raise after the flop out-of-position?"

"Tell me about it, Sam."

"I mean it's stupid. I didn't think anyone that dumb would still be left in the tournament. I just couldn't conceive of it."

"It's poker, Sam. Anything can happen."

"You're not doing a good job of cheering me up."

She finally took the shot by herself. She was tired of waiting for Owen. The shot didn't seem to make her feel any better. Screw alcohol. What she needed was something sweet. She picked up the menu looking for the desserts page. Owen was looking off in the distance. Again. At first she'd thought he was looking at a girl. But now she didn't know what the hell he was looking at. She didn't really care, either.

How did she lose concentration? That's the only thing she could think of. On the first day of the tournament, she would have already noticed the two clubs on the board when the third came down on the river. She would have noticed her opponent's huge stack and that he wasn't an idiot. She would have surmised that he was betting on the flush draw and had hit it. She would have folded. She kept telling herself she would have folded. Hmmm . . . the chocolate torte looks good.

The reason she hadn't noticed these obvious warning signs was quite simple, Sam thought—she was too tired. She was too tired because she couldn't sleep the night before. A wide-awake Sam would not have gone all-in. Not there. She could live with that excuse. Yeah. Chocolate torte.

Deep down, beneath a couple layers of Southern Comfort, a more sober Sam suspected that she had just failed to see the clubs because she didn't want to see them. She looked at Owen. He was still staring off.

"What's up with you?"

"What do you mean?"

"Why are you so quiet, Mr. Money?"

"Isn't that something? I swear, Sam, if I could switch places with you, I would. I'd give you my stack and let you bet for me."

"Well. That doesn't really do me much good, does it?" Silence. "No. Seriously. What's the matter? You arguing with the wife?"

"No. What makes you think that?"

"Just asking."

"Lisa is fine. Great, in fact. I haven't told her I advanced yet—just haven't had a chance to call."

Sam held up her glass. There was still a sip at the bottom.

"To your tournament."

"Yeah. Thanks."

"Okay, so why are you being such a mope then?"

A silence.

More silence.

Even more silence. Sam had had enough.

"Okay, Owen. What's your problem?"

"It's ReBicycle. That's my problem."

"I thought you said you didn't want to talk business."

"You asked me what I was thinking about."

"You said no business."

"You said no poker, but I just listened to that for 30 minutes."

"You win, Owen. Let's talk bikes."

"I'm not winning. I did the market research. Or the customer interviews or whatever. I spent all day talking to people."

"And?"

Owen took a moment. Sam looked around the bar. She had picked this place. It was only a couple of blocks from the hotel, close enough to stumble home but far enough away to feel like she had some distance from the tournament. They were seated at the corner of the bar, where they nearly faced each other but didn't have to. She wondered if the bartender thought they were on a date. Where was the bartender? Time to order that chocolate torte.

"Okay, I've been thinking about it all day—I think it's actually why I'm playing so well, I'm not overthinking poker like a lot of other people—but I've been thinking about what people told me yesterday."

"Wait. Who did you talk to, Owen?"

"I went to two bikes stores. The one in the hotel and the one where I rented my bike. All right. Two stores. Talked to almost 40 people. Some really in-depth. This one guy and I talked about the Tour de California for like 40 minutes. I listened to all of them.

And I asked them a lot of questions. About my assumptions. The stuff we talked about the other night. The best I could remember it. Not every detail, but you said break down the idea, get to the assumptions."

Had she said that? I mean, he was right, that's what he should do, but she didn't remember that.

"Okay."

"And my big assumption was that people want cheaper, quality bikes and that they would be willing to buy bikes online. I mean that's ReBicycle right there—good, affordable bikes online."

"So what did people tell you?"

"Well, they didn't care about price as much as I thought. Okay, whatever. I'm sure there are still a lot of bargain hunters out there."

"That's another assumption, Owen."

"Well, I'm going with it. But the news I can't get over is that nobody I talked to had bought a bike online. None. Zip. Zero. Some people had bought parts online. Some had looked online. But a full bike. A full road bike. The count was zero."

"And this news surprises you?" Now she was the one looking distracted, reading the drink menu trying to find the next liquid salvo she would fire across the bough of the USS Bad Beat.

"It's not what I was hoping for. More than surprise me, it shocks me. Like, the way you described the hand you went out on. That feeling of 'I can't believe this. How did I do this?' I had that feeling yesterday at the second bike store. Like I was finding out that I'd been betting chips into a losing hand all along. I was looking at a row of used bikes. Right in front of me. Not as nice as the ones we sell, but they were right there. And they had customers. Customers who bought two of those used bikes. In the four hours I was there, they sold two! I checked my Web stats from roughly the same time frame yesterday. Ten times as many people came through my site than through the physical store. Zero sales in that time frame. Zero!"

The bartender finally came. Sam was on the fence. She decided to change the theme of her pity party from liquor to junk food. "Hey, if I order dessert, will you eat half of it?" Owen shrugged.

Whatever, she needed something sweet. To the bartender, "Chocolate torte soufflé."

"The pastry chef makes each one individually. It takes around 20 minutes." The bartender was a fit, tan brunette. College aged with a small diamond stud on the left side of her nose. Sam caught Owen harmlessly noticing her.

"That's fine."

"With the raspberry sauce?"

"Yes please. And two coffees."

Owen spoke up. "No coffee. Beer for me. IPA. I don't care what type."

The bartender returned to the other side of the big, square bar where there were far more patrons. Sam turned back to Owen, who now seemed lost as to where he'd been.

"So to make a long story short, you realized the problem ReBicycle is trying to solve might not be a real problem."

"Okay. But do these customers really know what they want? I mean Steve Jobs never went out and interviewed anyone. And I think Henry Ford once said something like if he were to ask people what they wanted they would have said a faster horse."

Sam was trying to think of the raspberry sauce and not about the fact Owen just compared himself to Steve Jobs or Henry Ford. She would put it delicately. "Okay. Let me break my answer into two responses. First, let's talk about Henry. He's totally right. You can't ask people what they want. It's like I told you: People are terrible at predicting the future, and sometimes they plain out lie. But you can ask them about the past or the present. About current problems they are facing. And if Henry asked most people if they had pain about trying to find transportation to their jobs or to visit friends or family, people would have talked his ear off about all the different things they've tried to solve the problem."

Owen already looked defeated, but he made one more attempt at an argument. "Okay, and what about Jobs?"

"Great. Let's talk about Steve Jobs. Yes. He was a genius. Yes. He beautifully combined art and technology, but not all his guesses about what people wanted were right. The original Macintosh that Jobs created was a failure. I read that it didn't have a fan because Jobs thought it distracted from the calm of the computer and ended up frying all of the internal parts. The Lisa computer he created was also a failure. His next company, NEXT, created another personal computer that was a huge flop. But he had something like a hundred million dollars from his initial success and the ability to make lots of big bets without going broke. You don't have millions of dollars to bet on one idea after another, right?"

Owen begrudgingly nodded. "Right."

"So I'm trying to help you figure out a way to significantly de-risk your bet before you go all in. And the best way to do that is to make sure people want it before you spend too much time and money creating it. If you aren't solving a migraine problem, you need a lot of time and money to let people know that you are out there and convince them that they can benefit from your product. It's very expensive to convince people that they need or want something that they really don't."

Owen's beer finally came. He smiled at the bartender to thank her for the beer for what seemed like the first time he'd smiled all night and then immediately frowned again. Damn, when Sam first met him, he seemed so happy. That was five days ago. What had she done to him to make him this dour in so little time? Secretly, there must be a marriage problem. That was her theory. Not that she had thought it through . . . again with not thinking things through! No! Don't go there. Don't go back to the hand. Too late. Wait! There was the smile again. Owen was staring at her now with a smile on his face. Like staring really hard.

"What? Do I have food in my teeth?"

"No, I'm just hearing what you're saying. That I'm screwed."

"I didn't say that."

"But reading between the lines. ReBicycle is failing. My customers are people who buy bicycles. My business sells bicycles." He looked around conspiratorially. "It's okay, Sam. I've figured this out. As I was doing the interviews, I figured out what you said. It's not like you're breaking my heart."

"Oh, you did?"

"You're right. Misjudging a problem. That's what I've been doing. The customer exists. I know. I saw them in the store. But that's where I realized what the real problem is. You ready? ReBicycle is not an online store. It should be a physical store."

Oh, no. She could see where this was going. Fish out of water flailing around for dear life.

"I keep the same business model. Great bikes at a great price, but instead of selling where people aren't, I buy a cool shop, have a small sales staff, and make extra money doing repairs and maintenance. And every bike I sell on top of that is gravy. And, of course, I keep the web site up. Sell some bikes here and there. Gain word of mouth. Maybe sponsor a semi-pro team. Whatever. People start hearing about my shop. They look us up online and then they're like, 'Oh, they have a good web site. Oh, I can customize a bike and go look at it.' And that's how ReBicycle succeeds! Right? That's the answer."

There was a moment of quiet. Sam really wanted that raspberry sauce. She wanted Owen to stop trying to tweak the idea without research. She also wanted to tell Owen he was ass-backwards, but unlike the folks she had met as an investor, she didn't want to be there when he actually received the news.

"Would you be interested in investing in a business like that, Sam? I mean, I've done the research this time."

Wow. She didn't think it could get much worse, but it did. She needed to cut this off now. It was hard for her to put her thoughts together in this state, but she took a deep breath and tried to organize them as best she could.

"Look, Owen, remember when we talked about how a startup isn't a smaller version of a big company?"

"Sure."

"Well, a startup is just a temporary vehicle to find a good business model. Not just a problem and a solution, but an entire business model. That includes what kind of sales force you are going to use and how much they will cost, how you are going to get your supplies, how much your expenses are going to be, and finally, how much revenue you could possibly make from this business."

"Sam, we don't need to start at the beginning, I feel like I've proven over the last few . . ."

Sam turned her head and suppressed a burp.

"Listen, Owen. You are on tilt right now. You so badly don't want to consider ReBicycle a failure that you are just grasping for air looking for any kind of out. Opening a bike shop is, of course, a known commodity, but you still don't know if it's going to provide for your family or make the kind of revenue you are interested in. If I traveled back in time and asked the Owen who was still employed with a six-figure salary at the consulting firm, 'Fully employed Owen, how would you like to open a used bike shop?,' what would he say?"

Silence.

"He would say no, Owen. I don't doubt it."

Owen looked up from his beer, but he didn't speak. He pursed his lips and let them land somewhere between a grin and frown. That's his "Yeah, I guess so" face, she thought. She might be getting through.

"Do you remember why you started your company? What were you trying to do?"

"I wanted to build something bigger than myself. I wanted to create a company with a totally different culture than the consulting firm."

"Anything else?"

"I wanted the chance to make more money than I could working for someone else at the consulting firm."

"Those are all great reasons, Owen. But how can you possibly justify opening a bike shop when those are your motivators? How long would it take you to realize that the shop wouldn't solve any of your needs?"

"I just don't feel like I have the luxury of chasing dreams anymore. I need to be practical. I need to provide for my family."

"Well, taking on more debt to open a bike shop that may or may not pay you anything after all the expenses is not practical. It's desperate. That's all it is. It's me going all-in on that stupid hand when I should have already known I was going to lose and should have just folded to stay in the tournament."

Owen put his head down in his arms on the bar. She was definitely getting through to him.

"Look. **The ability to face failure and rejection is one of the greatest strengths of successful entrepreneurs**. What kind of poker player would you be if you never folded a hand? Your chips would run out in a hurry. And once you fold a hand, you can look forward to playing the next one. You have to play a lot of hands before you find an opportunity to win a big pot."

Owen didn't move.

"All you've figured out so far is that you aren't solving a migraine problem with your current model. And I don't know, 40 is a lot of people, but it's just the start. It's too narrow a subset of the population. Even assuming all these people are right and price doesn't matter and they don't buy online, that doesn't mean your business is outta whack; it just means your business doesn't resonate with a particular group of shoppers. You need to find some other group and talk to them. This is a huge marketplace. I feel like there are migraine problems in there to be solved, you just need to find them."

He looked up. "How?"

"You need to talk to more people. You've only been asking about price and how they shop. Maybe there are other migraine problems out there that you've neglected to find out about. The good news is that you've just won yourself a few more days in Vegas. You've got time to talk more broadly with people. Figure out what difficulties they are having in the bike buying process."

"Uhhhh."

Sam could see he was struggling with this. He just needed some encouragement.

"I've got a story, Owen, and I think you're gonna like it, my friend."

"Yeah. Is it about anything other than ReBicycle?"

"Yes, you can be off the hot seat for a minute."

"Is it about bicycles?"

Sam gave him a big smile, "Even better. It's about boobs."

Chapter 21

Test Your Assumptions before Committing Any Resources to an Idea

Owen didn't care about boobs. Well, that's not true, but tonight he didn't care about much of anything. The beer was kind of helping, but Owen had a migraine problem. Literally. He had a bad headache. Okay, not a migraine, but he wasn't feeling his best. He wanted to go to bed. He wanted to talk to Lisa. Sam was cool. Sam was fun to hang out with and not bad to look at. But tonight, Sam was not what he needed. He needed rest. Maybe not sleep but some Sportscenter, or a check up on what's been happening in the news. Have a dose of reality. It seemed like ever since he came here to Vegas to play poker, he had spent more time on nonpoker things. It was a back-and-forth. Business. Poker. Business. Poker. He couldn't keep his mind on one.

Like today. He'd woken up thinking about the business. In his dream, he was talking to some people like the interviews he had done yesterday when his wife Skyped him to say that the business had made its first $1.1 million. She held up a large check. Owen didn't know why it wasn't a cool million—maybe his subconscious gave an extra 10 percent interest for all his hard work. And why would a bicycle store ever have a huge check? Whatever the dream meant, it was definitely about the business. And as socially painful as the interviews were, he'd woken up wanting to do more. But he couldn't. He had to focus on poker. Twelve hours of it. From 8 A.M. to 8 P.M.

Earlier that morning, he had tried to engage people at his table about cycling—he was sure they were out there, and it was just a matter of luck of sitting next to one—but today wasn't the day. Everybody was too tense about the bubble.

And now after a full day of poker, Owen was trying to shift back to business. To ReBicycle. He should be excited about the $70,000 or so in winnings he was guaranteed after today's performance. That he was still in it. That he had a lot more money to win. But his cut of $35,000 was still just a drop in the bucket of what he owed to the bank and the credit card companies. Still. He should be celebrating, not feeling so sorry for himself.

When Owen returned Sam her car keys, he thought they were saying their final goodbyes. At least that's how the hug felt. Like a goodbye hug. He wished her good luck and she the same. But he had thought that while the chances were high he might not make it through day three, the strength of Sam's stack would easily carry her through the day. Another bad assumption. And now it was Owen who was still in the tournament and Sam was out. Funny how life works out sometimes.

And the funniest thing of all was that the more he talked with Sam and found out just how much trouble his business was in, the better he did in the tournament. It's like these talks kept him grounded.

"I'm game, Sam. Let's talk about your boobs."

"Not mine, Big Guy. My baby sister's."

"You don't have a sister."

"Yes, I do. I just haven't told you about her."

"Okay. So you have this younger sister. . . ."

"Right, so my sister, Val, had just had her first baby like four months before and she wanted to get away and have some fun. She came out to visit me in Chicago. She was still breastfeeding at the time, so she flew out for less than 24 hours. She landed at O'Hare, got a cab into the city, got to my place, unpacked her bags—and it turned out that somehow she forgot to pack her breast pump."

"Ohhh. I hate that!"

Sam punched his arm and laughed. "Shut up. I mean, she could have bought another one, but they cost hundreds of dollars. And she was so excited to go out and have some fun without being tethered to the baby and all the stuff that goes along with having a baby that she didn't do anything about it. And I didn't know any better, so we just took off. We went out and had a great time. We stayed out all night, basically. We even joked about how huge and awesome her boobs were. So the next day we got up late, ate some breakfast, and I put her in a cab back to the airport."

Owen's mind was starting to drift. They'd been talking business, and now Sam was off on some tangent. Must be the shots she'd ordered. Soco and lime. What a chick shot! He expected better of Sam. He'd expected her to make it past this day, too. He wondered how she played small pairs from early positions—limp in or fold? He'd been limping in but . . .

"Owen. Pay attention! This relates to ReBicycle."

Sam took another shot, leaned toward Owen, raised an eyebrow provocatively, and said, "It's about to get kind of graphic."

"I can take it," Owen smiled.

"Less than an hour later, Val called me from the airport. She was practically crying because she was in all this pain from not having pumped since before she left Denver. She felt like her breasts were about to burst, and there was nothing she could do. The pain was excruciating. She had tried pumping by hand, but that's apparently a lot trickier than you might think."

Owen had seen a breast pump once. A coworker had brought it into the consulting firm and he'd picked it up not knowing what it was at first. It scared him. Looked like two miniature suction cups hooked up to an ATV battery. Reason number 83 not to have kids.

"Okay. So she forgot her breast pump. Couldn't she just buy a new one?"

"Yeah. No! Apparently, they don't sell them at the airport! She was on the phone crying from all the pain."

"That doesn't sound good."

"No, it doesn't. So all of this was taking place before there was Internet on every phone in the world, so she called to have me Google some possible solutions. I went to my laptop and for the first time in my life searched for how to relieve milk-swollen breasts without a baby. You know what result one is? Right there on the preeminent home-parenting web site, it said apply ice or frozen cabbage."

"Okay."

"Oooooh." The bartender brought out Sam's chocolate dessert. A soufflé or something. It did look really good.

"Would you like another beer?"

Owen looked down. He hadn't even realized he'd finished the first one. That had gone quickly. Slow down, Owen. He declined. He'd have to take these parenting stories somewhat sober. But Sam's chocolate thingy did look good. He kept eyeing it.

"Do you want a bite?" Sam handed her fork to Owen. Ignoring the fact that they were now sharing silverware, he dove in. It was damn good.

"Okay. So where was I? Oh! Frozen cabbage. So the web site says apply frozen cabbage. I've never seen frozen cabbage in a grocery store. Much less an airport. Still with no frozen cabbage, she said she'd find some ice. Okay. Problem solved, I'm thinking. Fifteen minutes later, another phone call. No dice. She's still in pain. Back to the laptop. Looking up relieving swollen breasts for a second time. Second option was a hot compress. Not really doable at an airport. And so I went to option three, which was borrow a breast-feeding baby."

Owen kicked his head back and laughed. "What do you mean 'borrow'?"

"It means go up to a lady with a kid and ask 'Hey, is that a breastfeeding baby? Would you mind it if I borrowed him/her for a few minutes?' Now my sister is a strong, brave woman. She said she'd try it. Fifteen minutes later, she called back and told me she couldn't do it. It was too awkward. There were no good candidates. And she felt really uncomfortable about the whole thing."

"So what was option four?"

"Option four was find a slightly perverted businessman to breastfeed."

"Seriously?"

"I'm joking. There was no option four. Option four was to suffer. That's what my sister did. She got on the plane. Hungover. Giant breasts a' burstin' and she suffered through it."

Owen put his hand up to his chin and looked up at the ceiling to mime deep thought. "Mmmm. Yes. That was a good story, Sam. I look forward to turning ReBicycle around by always having extra breast pumps handy."

She punched him in the arm again. "Hey, you don't have to listen to part two of the story if you're bored."

"No, I'm sorry. I didn't realize there was more." He rubbed his arm. She was trying to be playful, but that kind of hurt.

"I know I've been drinking, but I'm not *that* drunk. Okay, don't get ahead of yourself. Don't get so excited looking for the river card and forget to the see the possible flush already on the board."

"What?"

"I was where you are. I thought I had found a problem worth solving. I thought that after helping my sister with her ordeal, there must be others who have similar experiences. That I could make a killing selling marked-up breast pumps at the airport. I thought it was a big idea."

She took another bite of dessert and chewed the way someone does when they're in a hurry to start talking again.

"So, the next few times I flew, I would show up to the airport a couple of hours early and walk around the terminal, talking to babies with mothers."

"You talked to babies?" Owen interjected with a laugh.

"Mothers with babies! I've had a few drinks, okay? Be gentle with me! Anyway, I asked if the *mothers* had ever forgotten their pumps. I was very disappointed with the results. Nobody had ever had the same problem. I mean, some of them would say they'd forgotten their pump, or the pump stopped working, but they would just buy another one in whatever city they were visiting."

"Yeah, I know that feeling of disappointment well."

"But I didn't stop just by asking them about their breast pumps. That would have been really limiting. I mean, my original assumption was wrong. But I checked it out before I committed any resources to it. And while I was interviewing these women, I made sure to listen to what they had to say. I didn't try to convince them that Val's problem was their problem. And once I started asking them about the difficulties of traveling with babies, there wasn't a shortage of problems for us to talk about. And so even though airport breast engorgement wasn't some hidden terror traumatizing traveling mothers, those women did seem to run out of a lot of baby-related accoutrements in their travels. I mean, you name it: diapers, wipes, formula, diaper rash ointment, bibs, burp cloths, dry onesies. And it was a real problem when flights got delayed or canceled because maybe they put all their stuff in their checked bags because they didn't think they'd need it for their short flight, but then suddenly they have three or four extra hours at the airport. Or they have to go to some airport hotel for the night. People told me stories of some very creative things that they had done to create makeshift baby products they desperately needed."

"So you found a new problem worth solving?"

"Yes! And whenever I'd be at an airport, I'd go to whatever general store or mall they had and, sure, some had baby food and some had bibs and diapers, but there were no baby-related stores in any mall. None!" She was starting to slur the occasional word.

"What about the vending machines I see with all the baby stuff in it?"

"You mean Flybaby? Well, that's the point of this entire story. Of the swollen boobs. Flybaby. That's my baby."

Owen suddenly felt focused. "Wait! You started that baby vending machine company?"

"It's called Flybaby."

"I've seen Flybaby! It's brilliant. My wife points them out whenever she sees them."

"Yep, all thanks to my sister's migraine problem." As Sam said this, she held both hands in front of her chest to make the international gesture for big breasts.

"Why didn't you tell me you started Flybaby before?"

"Are you kidding? It barely grossed $10 million last year. Sparksys grossed a hundred-something mil. Not that I'm involved in either anymore. I started five pilot Flybaby spots, made deals with a bunch of airports, and then sold the rights."

"Wow, Sam. You are full of surprises!" Owen snatched the fork from her hand and scooped up a bite of her dessert. He was impressed. While he didn't know Flybaby by name, once she described it, he knew instantly what company she was talking about.

As Sam told him of her trips to Asia—where, she said, vending machines were used much more widely and creatively—Owen considered the enormity of Sam's "obvious" and "simple" idea. It was much bigger than that, he thought. This was something that improved people's lives. A business that could solve a real-world problem. Sam was changing the world. A diaper-dispensing vending machine wasn't a cure for cancer, but neither was polyester or the iPhone. But they were improvements, all the same. They changed the world for the better. Good lord, who the hell was this chick?!

Sam seemed to find elegant solutions to bona fide problems everywhere she turned. It was electrifying to Owen. He wanted to do the same kinds of things, but he was growing increasingly doubtful that ReBicycle was the way to get there. He had been flailing around with his germ of an idea for a year, and only now was he starting to realize what he hoped to accomplish with it. He wanted to help people solve problems. Unfortunately, he'd gone about it backwards: he came up with an elegant solution before he'd spotted a problem.

But he also realized, to his surprise, that he didn't care if the problem he'd assumed existed was real or not. Because somewhere in his stockpile of discarded bike components and bent frames, there was bound to be a solution to a problem that was important to cyclists. And, if so, he only had to dig in and find out what it was.

Sam's approach to starting a business—finding a problem worth solving and finding a solution the market wanted—was making a lot of sense. It inspired him. He had never known anyone who talked about business this way. An idea. It was turning an idea into a business that inspired Owen to leave the consulting world and start ReBicycle. He had tried and failed to explain that to people, especially to Lisa. Some people aren't wired to understand how turning the idea of selling diapers and baby formula from bright pink-and-blue vending machines would be more satisfying than working on a billion-dollar acquisition or a Fortune 500 company's restructuring.

But Sam understood it. She was living that life, the one that Owen had envisioned for himself, and Owen was mesmerized by the details of it. He could safely say that he had never connected with anybody in this way. Maybe it was hero worship. Maybe it was the (four? five?) drinks. He couldn't deny that he was drawn to her. The realization made him very uncomfortable, very quickly. He pushed his chair back and put both his feet solidly on the floor. He tried to make himself still to gauge his intoxication.

"How was the dessert?" It was the bartender.

"It was damn good."

"Wonderful. Can I get some more drinks for you?"

Owen looked at his watch. Nearly midnight. He needed sleep. But he wanted to hear more. He could do another . . .

"I'm ready for the check." Sam beat him to it. Fortunately for Owen, sexism carried the day and the bartender laid the check down in front of Owen and Sam didn't have a chance to grab it. He finally felt as though he had the dough to cover it, thanks to the World Series.

There was a chill in the air as they were walking from the restaurant to the hotel—the desert cools down quickly after the sun drops. The neon and flash just makes it look like it should be a lot warmer than it is in Vegas. Sam had only worn a tank top. She must be freezing. As they were walking, she shivered and moved in close. For warmth, Owen! She's just cold, Owen, don't make it weird.

Owen's mind went to a conversation he once had with Lisa about infidelity. He remembered her asking how they were going to avoid the same fate as so many couples they had known whose relationships had gone sour. They did seem to know a handful of people who had found themselves faced with temptation and had made bad decisions. The answer, Owen had said with confidence, was not putting yourself in proximity to temptation in the first place. Temptation doesn't just spring on you. It happens gradually, bit by bit, so that it doesn't seem like anything all that dangerous is happening until suddenly all the sand is through the hourglass and you're out of time.

It's probably best that this evening is about to come to a close. He wasn't sure if he would ever see Sam again. She'd likely leave town now that she was out of the tournament. He just had one more burning question he had to ask.

As they approached the hotel entrance, he spoke, "Hey, Sam. I've got a question for you."

Poking him in the left pectoral with her finger, she answered, "What's up, Big Fella?"

"You think I can fix ReBicycle? Like if you took over running it tomorrow, would you have a handful of things you'd immediately change?"

"Owen, I haven't the faintest clue what I'd do. Neither do you right now. But you're finally on the right trail to figuring it out.

Focus on the customers. Figure out if there's a migraine problem out there. Unfortunately for you, it's not as easy as new mothers at airports. And I don't know who the customer is. Neither do you. But you'll figure it out."

"Yeah, I will." Owen was feeling a little cocky for some reason. He knew there was no good reason for it. Time for bed. But before he could say anything . . .

"You wanna grab another drink, Owen?" They were walking past a hotel bar.

Yes. The thought manifested quickly.

No. That was definitely a bad move.

He didn't really want another drink. He needed sleep. But the dinner. The advice. The walk back. He just wasn't ready for it to end. That feeling had to be wrong.

"I don't think that's a good idea. I think I need some rest for play tomorrow."

"Oh yeah, rub it in, why don't you!?"

"I didn't mean to . . ."

"It's fine. I'm okay with it. Goodnight, you big bicycle stud you." She stopped walking just short of the elevators and spread out her arms for a goodbye hug.

They hugged. They kept hugging. Sam laid her head on his chest for a moment.

"Owen, good luck tomorrow." She looked up at him with her pretty green eyes. She kept the eye contact.

And then she kissed him.

Chapter 22

Luck Can Be Engineered if You Take Emotion Out of the Equation

"So you fill it out. Put down your age, hometown. What you do. Any interesting facts about yourself like you got 10 kids or you collect snakes. You know, something that makes you stand out. Last year one guy put that all he ever wore was plaid. For good luck, ya know? Seems stupid, but he made the final 20 and guess what?—got a sponsorship from a plaid-shirt company. Ya never know."

Owen looked around. There were about 30 or so competitors around him. All looking intently at the sheet of paper in their hand or the man speaking. He was a producer from ESPN, and while he didn't say it outright, they knew what he meant. The tournament had finally narrowed down to enough players that the cameras would start focusing on individuals rather than random exciting hands throughout the tournament. There were now few enough players that ESPN could start developing TV personalities for individual players, build them a fan base, and generally increase ESPN's viewing audience.

"You wanna know how you make it on the tube?" The man continued, "I tell people the same thing every year. Be loud enough and last long enough. You got 10 minutes to fill it out. Even if you don't want to be on TV, we still need your name and hometown. Any questions?"

There were a couple of people who raised their hands. Owen immediately zoned them out and focused on the sheet. He wasn't sure whether he wanted to be on television. He laughed to himself. He had spent much of the last year trying to get any kind of media attention he could for ReBicycle. He thought about how excited Owen from a year ago would be to have his company name and schwag all over ESPN. Now, he didn't really have much use for it.

Frankly, he still couldn't believe he'd even made it this far in the tournament. It all seemed like a dream. After his round yesterday, everything had been a blur. First, there was the news of Sam's elimination right on the bubble. While he'd never tell her this, he was partially happy it happened.

He realized now that it made him focus on something other than the cards. Owen was smart enough to recognize his own worst tendencies, and the absolute worst was to become emotional about the cards, to rationalize why stupid moves might work out because he thought he was smarter than his opponent or he really needed the hand to work out. His best plays came when his mind was somewhat distracted, when he could just be objective and play the odds rather than become too emotionally invested in the hands. And Sam's exit had been a helpful distraction.

Fortunately, there had been a lot of helpful distractions during the first rounds of the tournament. ReBicycle alone was responsible for much of Owen's wandering thoughts. It sometimes felt like he wasn't focusing enough on the cards. Then there was Sam. She'd been another distraction. Now, Owen could already feel his heart beating at an accelerated pace. It would be tougher to keep finding healthy distractions. The stakes were too high. The producer and his worksheet weren't helping.

Owen wrote down the easy stuff. Name, age, hometown. Then came profession. Should he put entrepreneur? Businessman? Tech owner? Maybe that was Owen's problem. He couldn't figure out what ReBicycle was. Forget it. This isn't the time to overanalyze it. He put down bike-shop owner. Close enough. Then came hobbies. Owen left that blank. What was he even doing with the rest of the form? This form, the cameras, they were psyching him out. He left the rest of it blank.

Owen turned in the form to the producer who was wearing a Red Sox cap and was the only one who didn't look a little nervous. He quickly skimmed Owen's answers, his eyes darting around the page.

"You own a bicycle shop?"

"Yeah."

"Cool. You used to race?"

"In college."

"But not pro?"

"I wish."

"You know Lance Armstrong?"

"Just what I've seen on TV."

The guy took one more look at Owen. Whatever he was looking for, he quickly decided Owen didn't have it.

"Okay then. We'll be in touch."

There was a queue building up behind Owen. The next guy up was an older gentleman he didn't recognize in a cowboy hat. As Owen was leaving, he overheard the guy say in a thick Texas drawl that he had never been to Vegas, he had used his lotto winnings to enter the tournament on a whim, and never played this fancy Hold 'Em version of poker before. As Owen was getting out of earshot, the Texan was describing how he'd rubbed his favorite steer's horns for luck before getting on the plane. Owen didn't have to look behind him to know that the producer was grinning. This guy was good TV.

Really, though, Owen was grinning, too. That Texan meant that Owen was still not the biggest novice left in the tournament. He was worried that he might be. He definitely felt lucky to make it this far, but there was a nagging feeling inside him that it had been too easy—really, a couple of lucky breaks, a couple of good runs of cards, and keeping a low-profile the rest of the time had helped him make it to the money.

But it wasn't just luck. He knew that. Owen thought back to his conversation with Sam about slot machines versus poker. He wasn't just coasting through this tournament on luck alone. He was taking very calculated risks, minimizing his potential exposure on hands, and continuously analyzing his chances in a hand based on new information. Owen wasn't worrying about money already committed to a hand, he was thinking about his odds moving forward. He wasn't gambling. He was excelling at a game of skill because he minimized his risks and, yeah, gotten lucky a time or two. But he had also had some bad luck during the tournament. He was still in because he was able to make sure his losses didn't cripple him. Now, though, guys like the 10-gallon hat cowboy would be few and far between. There were virtually no gamblers left. The vast majority of the 244 players remaining were extremely skilled, and by the end of today, their number would dwindle to 85.

With 30 minutes to go before play began for the day, Owen was thinking about how to keep himself distracted. Keep his mind off poker. The cell phone came out. The last number he had dialed had been Sam. Nope. She's gone. Gone. Gone. Gone.

Oooh. Better idea. Owen dialed Lisa.

"Lisa Chase."

"Well, hello, Mrs. Chase. This is Mr. Chase." Owen always found it amusing that his wife would pick up the phone at school with that greeting.

"Hey, Owen. I'm auditing a class. Can we talk later?"

"Hey. Yes or no. Can you get someone to cover for you the rest of the week?"

"I don't know, what's up?"

"You know how you asked me how much money I've won? Well, now I've definitely won a lot. Like a lot, a lot. And I could win a lot more today. Or not. But either way, you should come join me here. We should take some time to get away and celebrate."

Pause.

"Owen, do you know how much it would cost for me to . . ."

"Honey, I'm up a lot of money. We can afford it, I promise. This could be the vacation you've been waiting to take. And I could really use you here."

"I don't know if I can just leave for the rest of the week."

"Look, just give it some thought. I think having you here would really help me play better. And we could use the time away."

It was the perfect idea. Lisa had fallen for a younger, more unpredictable, wilder version of himself, and this was definitely unexpected. She had to be excited about this opportunity.

"Owen, I . . ."

"Honey, I've got to go play. Please find a ticket online. It doesn't matter how much it costs." He was hoping that if he rushed her into it, it would help her make the decision faster. He knew that she wanted to do it—she just needed a little push.

"Owen, I'm not coming."

That was oddly firm. And a little cold. Owen didn't expect that kind of reaction. Maybe he needed to ease off the gas a little.

"Come on, honey, just talk to some of the others and see if they can cover—"

"Owen, I'm not coming because I don't want to."

"What?" He was confused.

"I didn't want to upset you while you were doing so well, so I hadn't said anything, but our conversation the other night really bothered me."

"What do you mean?"

"I just don't think you can ever give this up. I mean, it seems like you've got a taste for this entrepreneur thing or whatever it is, and you just don't want to let it go. You just want to do more. Like I look at the last year and say, wow, we tried that and it didn't work, time to go back to the real world and get a job, maybe start a family, and you don't see it that way at all. You've got the bug for this stuff something bad, and it's great that you are so passionate, but I don't know if that's the kind of life I want."

Owen found a staged sofa chair in the hotel lobby and sat down. He was trying to wrap his mind around what Lisa was trying to say. He wasn't sure, but he knew this wasn't good. He felt the air leave the room.

"Lisa, what are you saying?"

"I'm not saying anything, Owen. I just need some time to think."

"About what?"

"About the kind of life I want, and how I might fit into yours."

"Lisa, come on . . ."

"I gotta go, Owen. I'll talk to you soon. Good luck today. Really."

"Lisa, wait!"

But she was gone.

Owen slowly pulled the phone from his ear, perhaps hoping that she would jump back on the line, knowing full well that wasn't technologically possible. This wasn't good.

He checked the time. Twenty-two minutes before play was starting.

Well, at least he had found his new distraction.

Chapter 23

Every Successful Entrepreneur Has More Failures than Successes

"What do you mean you don't have any flights out of Vegas?!?"
Sam slammed down her head on the ticket counter.
She wondered for a split second if she was overdoing it.
Nope, better to err on being too dramatic and get a supervisor over
who could bump her to the front of the standby list.

"I need to fly out today!"

"Hmmm . . ." The agent pretended to type something into the
computer. At least that's what Sam had always suspected they did—
that the screen was really just blank. "Ma'am, I'm sorry. Everything
in and out of Chicago is canceled."

"What do you mean canceled?"

"The weather . . . up to four inches."

"Four inches of what?"

"Rain, ma'am. Lots of lightning in the area."

"I can get you to Milwaukee tomorrow evening and then you'd be on standby to Chicago."

"Tomorrow evening?"

"I'm sorry, ma'am, but even before the delays, we were very full. This is the week of the World Series of Poker."

More slamming of head on counter. This time in earnest. She didn't need to be reminded of the World Series. That she went out on the bubble. That she kissed Owen.

"Are you serious?"

"Tomorrow evening, ma'am. Milwaukee is your best bet."

The agent actually turned the computer around so Sam could look at it. It was full of red type. It didn't take a rocket scientist to realize this wasn't a good thing.

"When's the earliest flight to Chicago?"

"Tomorrow."

"Okay. I want that one."

"It's at 5:45 A.M., and you'll be number 10 on the standby list."

"Jesu—" Don't curse at her. She's just doing her job. Deep breaths. Change tactics. Take a look at her nametag. Annette. Sell Annette on helping you, Sam.

"Annette, when's the earliest no-shit, I have a seat and I'm flying, flight I can get?"

Annette swiveled the screen back around so Sam couldn't see it. Apparently she didn't appreciate cursing. A little more typing and then a very forced smile.

"Seven P.M. two days from now. Is there someone you can spend some extra time with while you're still in Vegas?"

Ha. Sam couldn't believe she went in for that kiss. No, that's not true. She wanted to kiss him. She just couldn't believe that he turned his face to turn it into a cheek kiss.

Sam closed her eyes. She tried replaying the moment. It only replayed in slow motion. She'd gone in for the kiss— she didn't mind being the aggressor. All going according to plan, until she hit cheek, when she was perfectly sure she had aimed for lips. Bad assumption, Sam! He must have quickly turned his head when he saw it happening. Yep, total fail on her part. She'd misread the situation. That's what happens when you try to kiss a married man. What was she thinking?

"I'll take the ticket."

Annette was printing off the new ticket before Sam had even finished her sentence.

"Here's your ticket, ma'am. 7 P.M."

"Thanks."

One last forced smile from Annette.

"And again we do apologize for the delays."

Sam now had a couple of choices. She quickly decided against another rental car—what with the World Series, it'd probably be a nightmare to get one of those without a reservation. So she was taking a taxi, but where to? Not having a car meant getting a place within walking distance of the WSOP.

Going back to the Rio was the only thing that made sense—she stayed there every time she came to Vegas, and she knew the spa was world class, not to mention she still had a keycard that let her into the hotel's exclusive pool.

The more she thought about it, she could only find two reasons not to go there—it'd be awkward to run into Owen, and it would be awkward to go back to the place where she'd just gotten knocked out of the World Series of Poker—on the bubble! But she was strong enough to deal with both. She was sure of that.

Well, she was almost sure.

Chapter 24

The Harder You Work, the Luckier You'll Get

Something had changed about the tournament by Round 4. If the first three rounds had reminded Owen of Darwin's Law and to stay out of the way, the fourth round, and seventh full day of poker, reminded him of the one time he'd raced a Formula 1 car. Like all men, Owen considered himself an expert driver and had jumped at the chance when his company sponsored a fun day at a track with F-1s. He had fun but also found the experience terrifying—everything was going so fast that there was virtually no time to react. Curves came up in a split second and you had to go from 150 to 75 mph in an instant. It was thrilling. It was exhilarating. And there was no room for error.

The poker hands were now going just as fast. The bets just as big, like the speedometer in the car, and there was no time to think.

Owen had to slow it down. This wasn't healthy. He had to think through his decisions and evaluate his odds at each turn.

As he tried to evaluate an early hand, he thought about how fast life at ReBicycle had seemed these past few months. He was no longer the calm, organized professional who had started the company what seemed like years ago. Once he figured out that ReBicycle wasn't performing anywhere close to his financial projections, Owen frantically tried anything he could to get back on track. But the money he spent on marketing gimmicks, PR campaigns, and web site redesigns wasn't producing any noticeable results. He was just spending money at a faster and faster rate, hoping to get lucky. It was clear to Owen now. Rather than speed up, he needed to slow things down. He now understood the value of getting paying customers before investing a lot of time and money. It just gave you so much more room to think and try new things.

He was staring at an 8-7 of hearts. An ordinarily easy hand to lay down, but he realized he was right behind the big blind and in the dealer position. Being in the dealer position meant he would be able to see what everyone else was doing before he had to act; that is, everybody else would bet or fold before him and then he could bully them around by throwing a huge amount into the pot. Play the players, not the cards, Owen said to himself.

Owen placed the minimum bet and thought about the power of the dealer position. As he watched the other players around the table posture to convey their positions, he decided that this level of information was the equivalent of gathering actual customer feedback before getting too far down the road in building his company. If you could pick any starting position in a poker hand, you would always pick the dealer spot because of all the added intel you could gather from the other players before you had to act. Why wouldn't you do the same in a new venture? **Interviewing your potential customers and learning about their actual problems and needs gives you a much more powerful starting position than guessing about those needs on your own.**

Five players decided to enter the hand—a large number for this far into the tournament. They'd been playing for several hours already, and the adrenaline from making it this far was starting to wear off. Owen could tell a couple of the guys in the hand were stifling yawns or drinking Red Bulls. It was going to be a long afternoon. The dealer looked the most bored of everybody. She took one look around the table and laid the flop down.

"Eight of spades. 8 of clubs. 7 of spades. Play to the big blind."

Owen stifled a yawn. At least he tried to make it look like he was stifling a yawn. In reality, his heart had almost burst out of his chest cavity. Forget the flush he was hoping for—he'd flopped a full house. The best hand! The nuts! It was the type of hand that comes around only once a tournament—if you're lucky.

That's just it, Owen thought. **If you spend time trying to gather intelligence, every now and then, you'll get lucky and strike gold!**

Owen played the hand carefully. He wanted to get as much cash out of it as he could, and that meant not letting anyone on to the incredible hand he was holding. After several rounds of bets, Owen was able to get the pot to $200,000. A healthy addition to his chip stack. The table had let out a collective gasp when he turned over his cards. It took a serious player to play an 8-7 this far into the tournament. At least that was the general impression. Owen knew better. This had more to do with the dealer position than the strength of his hand. Pitchford would have been very proud. Lisa would even be impressed.

Urhhh . . . Lisa. As Owen shoveled his winnings toward his seat and began to stack them into organized denominations, he thought about the fact that Lisa still hadn't returned any of his texts. He decided to step away from the table and send her an e-mail.

Lisa,

I'm so sorry about our conversation the other night. We were both tired and said a lot of weird things. I'm really sorry. I think we need to see each other in person. I think that'll fix all of this. It's the distance that's likely causing most of this angst.

We can afford the ticket. Really! No matter what it costs! We could really benefit from the time together in a fresh spot.

I love you. Please let me know that you're okay.

Love,

Sandy

He smiled at the signature line as he hit send. In his years of consulting, he and Lisa often found themselves sending each other little notes throughout the day over e-mail, before text messaging was a thing. One day, Lisa sent a really sweet note and signed it Patty. She said she was bored of always signing her e-mails with her name, and she wanted a new creative conclusion to the e-mail. So she started making up all sorts of new names, and as silly as this practice was, it made Owen smile at the end of every e-mail. And he quickly followed suit. Signing his e-mail Sandy was just a small way to let her know how much he cared and an attempt to remind her of the good times they used to have at the beginning of their relationship when their biggest problem was finding opportunities to be together.

That seemed like such a long time ago. Owen was worried about Lisa. She seemed so down about this business. It was weird. She was so supportive at first, but it was as though she didn't understand what startup life meant. Who was he kidding? He himself had no idea what startup life held in store for him.

Owen started walking back to the table when, out of the corner of his eye, he saw a blond ponytail going in the opposite direction. For a second he almost yelled out Sam's name before coming to his senses. What was his subconscious trying to tell him if he was still imagining Sam in every blond chick he saw out of the corner of his eye? He shook it off and headed back.

Chapter 25

Opportunities to Find Prospective Customers Are Everywhere—You Just Have to Look

B ack at the table, Owen was thinking about the idea he'd had for a retail store. Sam had shot that down pretty quickly, and Owen realized she was right. But what scared him was how much he believed in the idea before she shot it down. He was being desperate again and trying to find a panacea, when what he really needed was to slow down, put himself in a stronger position, and gather information from actual customers.

Owen promised himself that he was done dreaming up solutions on his own. That he was going to get customers first before committing to any new fixes. That he was going to stop throwing money behind bad cards, hoping to get lucky. No more gambling, Owen!

As if on cue, Owen received some great new cards. Ace-king. Was this a sign that he was headed in the right direction? Was the universe trying to reward him for finally seeing the error of his ways with ReBicycle?

"Hey, Biker-Boy, you gonna play today?"

It was James, an Asian NYU grad student who had spent the entire day at Owen's table. Owen found James's question very odd because James didn't normally talk in hands in which he was playing. Also, he hadn't called Owen Biker-Boy before. He definitely had some good cards. Or he had absolutely nothing and was bluffing. No in-between.

"How you know I'm into bikes?"

"Everybody knows. That one chick said you raced with Lance Armstrong."

"What chick?"

"Blonde chick."

One of the other players, Philip, a contractor from Chicago who had already folded, decided to add his two cents.

"Look at him. Acting like he doesn't know who we're talking about. I know your girlfriend is a spy."

"She's not my girlfriend. I'm married. Happily married."

James laughed.

"That's what they all say . . . I raise."

James pushed a sizable chunk of his stack into the middle. If the cycling talk was meant to distract Owen, it was working.

"What did she say about me cycling?"

Philip was first to respond, "She said you raced with Lance Armstrong."

"Really?"

"And you owned a bike business . . . big bike business. I almost approached you earlier in the tournament when she pointed you out. My fiancé is big into that stuff, you know? Trying to get me into it."

Owen hadn't really thought about people like Philip and James as prospective customers, but maybe this entire time, there'd been a great section of people to talk to right in front of him. Why hadn't Sam said anything? Action was back to him. It was just him and James. Focus. With A-K there was only one hand you fold to pre-flop. Ace-ace. Owen took a good long stare at James. James noticed and stared back.

"You know my brother loves bikes." James was nervously playing with his remaining chips. It was clear that if Owen called, James would have to go all-in on this hand.

"Yeah, James? A lot of people's brothers' love bikes."

James smiled slightly.

"My brother is here. He buys bikes all the time. You should meet him."

Something about the way James smiled and tried to appease Owen turned him off. Owen folded his ace-king.

James turned over ace-ace.

Eight months later, when the tournament was finally broadcast on ESPN, the announcers would label this the second-best fold of the tournament. Owen didn't know any of that right now. All he knew was that smile had scared him and he wanted to meet this brother, if this brother actually existed. More than that, though, he needed to open up and see what his fellow players thought about cycling while he had the free focus group at the poker table. For the first time, he felt genuinely excited to interview these potential customers, no matter the results. He had to try to find a true pain. A problem worth solving. He had finally stopped selling and started asking, and he was thrilled just to know the difference.

Chapter 26

The Best Feedback from Potential Customers Comes from Meticulous Interviews

"So today on the show we're talking to Crossfit champion Kyle Jevos about his new book on finding the GPS to the G-sp—"

Click.

"This bulldog's name is Sophie and she and her owners, Laura and Nathan, originally hail from Meers, Colorado, just outside of Boulder. Coincidentally, the last bulldog to win—"

Click.

"A popular 'Twitter comedian' who spends his days as a corporate lawyer? We'll introduce you to the always obscene Walker Adams later this hour, but first—"

Click.

"Keep it tuned right here on—"

Click. Off.

Sam threw the remote off the bed. She'd canceled her cable subscription a couple of years ago and didn't regret it. This junk was a good reminder of that smart decision.

She looked at the clock. 6:30 P.M. Her stomach rumbled. She'd been cooped up inside the hotel since leaving the airport. She had settled for the one-hour seaweed bath at the spa—their only available opening that day—and a 30-minute run at the gym. That was pretty much it. She needed something to eat. She'd hardly eaten all day.

Sam had spent enough time on the road to understand the golden rule of eating alone—that when you're full of self-confidence and eagerness, you're never really eating alone. Sure, you may be sitting at a bar stool alone but your inner self doesn't care. It's like its own separate person, and people somehow pick up on that. However, when a person is down or lonely or just not in the right state of mind, there's nothing worse than to eat by yourself. All it does is magnetize the loneliness.

Sam looked at her cell phone again. No new alerts. She'd texted a friend in Vegas an hour ago, but he was still at work.

Screw it. Time to go and explore. She ditched the sweatpants and put on her favorite pair of jeans and her form-fitting True Religion T-shirt. She was already feeling better. Now, where to go?

She needed some place to escape for a while, where she didn't know what she'd see. As she got into the elevator, Sam saw the floor below the ground floor labeled "Mezzanine Shops." This was the hotel's answer to retail, and surprisingly Sam had yet to visit. She pressed the button for the mezzanine level. At the very least she knew (based on overheard conversations from some of the poker players) that there was a pizza place at the south end of the shops that served unbelievable wood-fired, Neapolitan-style pizza by the slice. With only one day left in Vegas and no set plans, she could do a lot worse than some world-class pizza.

If someone were to try to describe Vegas to an outsider, the indoor/outdoor mezzanine mall at the Rio would be a good place to start. When Sam first walked out of the elevator she thought for a split-second that she had stepped outside. After all, it was overwhelmingly bright and the sky was a perfect blue. It was at least a couple of solid seconds before she realized she was looking at a painting of the sky, probably 50 to 60 feet in the air above her head. Simulating the sunlight were lights in pretty much every place she looked, but not in any kind of obnoxious way.

The mall was laid out in a series of tentacles. As Sam made her way down the street that led to the pizza place, and it really did feel like walking down a street, she noticed that the stores that lined the sidewalk were straight out of a fashion catalog. Burberry, Zara, Prada, Rodarte, Jimmy Choo's. If somebody in *Sex in the City* had worn it, it was here. Smattered among all these high-end stores were the type of stores you could find at any good ol' Mall USA. Footlocker, a Nike store, a high-end candy store, and, yes, even a bicycle store.

Sam didn't even realize she had stopped in front of the bike store until after a few seconds had passed. Window shopping had a tendency to make her daydream, and Sam was deep in thought about a hand in the tournament. Not *the* hand, but an earlier hand she'd also lost. It was nothing important. What was important, or at least significant in some way, is that she had unconsciously stopped in front of this bicycle store. There was only one frame in the window. It was bright red with some Italian word she didn't recognize painted on the side. Beautiful. No other way to describe it. Absolutely sleek and gorgeous.

How had she not looked at a real-life bicycle in the past three or so days while she'd been talking about them? Is this what it was all about? If so, the curves of the frame, the glistening paint—it was like a Ferrari on two wheels. And right below it was a sign Sam couldn't believe. The sign was in a bronze color and simply had two words: "8 pounds." It could only mean the frame she was looking at, but she couldn't believe that. Her first laptop had weighed eight pounds! She could still remember lugging her bike in middle school up the stairs at the school entrance and how she'd get winded after only a few steps . . . how much did that bike weigh? It was ridiculous. Eight pounds? There was no way!

Sam's gaze shifted from the bike to the gentleman on the other side of the glass looking at the bike. If he noticed Sam, he didn't show it. He was focused on the frame. Then another frame. Then another frame after that. If Owen had a brother who was a couple of years younger, had an earring and a more developed upper body, this guy would have fit the bill. It was clear he was into bikes. He had a couple of pamphlets in his hand but Sam couldn't tell if he'd picked them up at the store or brought them with him.

For the next 10 minutes, the guy in the bike store followed a similar pattern: Look at the frame in the window. Pick up a black frame in the store. Inspect it. Put it down. Pick up a red frame next to it. Look at the frame window again. Pick up the black frame in the store again. Pick up the red frame next to it. Rinse. Repeat.

For some reason Sam couldn't stop watching this take place. She was enthralled with this guy, and it was clear that he was trying to choose among the three frames. Secretly, she was rooting for the one in the window. She didn't know if it was the best or if it cost the most, but it was the one he couldn't pick up and try and that made it the underdog, which made it easy to root for. But then, after staring at the frame in the window for an extra-long period of time (and getting Sam's hopes up), the guy left without saying a word. Not even goodbye to the attendant in the bike shop.

Again, without really realizing it, Sam started following him to see what he would do next. It was like a secret mission. Something in those bikes had turned him off, and she wanted to know what it was. Even if she was never going to talk to Owen again, she had to know what was going through this guy's mind.

What was he going to do now? Sam thought he was probably shopping around. Maybe he'd head to the sporting goods store in one of the other mall arteries or just continue shopping for something else. No! Instead, the man walked all the way down to the food court. He bypassed all the high-end options, including the

Neapolitan place Sam was planning on enjoying later and ended up at a Panda Express. How depressing. Sam was now right behind him in line. She waited until he was seated to make her move. Rule number 17 of customer interviews: **People sitting down are more likely to talk and endure questions than people walking or standing.** It's just harder for them to get away.

"Excuse me. Do I know you from somewhere?"

The man looked at Sam and after a second shook his head. Little pieces of fried rice came flying out of his mouth. Sam ignored that, "No. I definitely know you from somewhere."

"I was in the World Series of Poker."

"No . . . that's not it. I haven't seen you there . . . no. I think it was at a race. Are you a racer? You look like it."

"A race? Are you sure it was me?"

"Or a cycling event. You know, around a track outdoors. No. I've definitely seen you there."

Finally, the man lit up, "Oh. The Crit Course. Yeah, I do race in the Crit races. So you've seen me race?"

"Almost 100 percent positive. And I think I just saw you at the bike store, too." Rule number 3: **Always qualify your interviews to make sure they are the customer segment you are targeting and not just a random person.**

"Yep. I was there."

Sam took a seat across from the man. She didn't ask for permission. She was going down a rabbit hole and determined to chase it now that she had a tail.

"What were you doing at the bike store?" Rule number one: **Ask open-ended questions to get them talking.** The more comfortable they are, the more they'll be willing to share.

"What do you mean? I was looking at bikes."

"To buy?"

"Who knows? Gotta convince the wife first."

"Mhhmmm." This was Sam's way of stalling. Finally, she figured out what she wanted to ask him, "Okay, I'm going to cut to the chase—I'm Sam, by the way."

"Brian."

"So, Brian, a friend of mine is in the bike biz. You've probably never heard of his company—"

"Look. I'm sorry but I'm not really interested in buying anything right now."

Shit. Rule number five: **Potential customers will be a lot more open about their problems if you don't try to sell them something during the initial interview.**

"I'm not selling you anything, Brian. I promise. Really. I'm just trying to help a friend answer some questions about people who buy road bikes. Listen, do you drink?" A nod, "Hold on." A few minutes later Sam came back from the faux Bier Garden Place and positioned a beer in front of Brian. "Here. All you gotta do is answer a few questions for me."

"Okay." Brian took the beer. Sam sat back down across from him and leaned into the table. It was the same sitting stance she took when she was trying to read an opponent. But first a quick drink from her beer."

"That is some good beer," she said.

"Yeah. I've been going there after dinner for the last couple nights of the tournament."

"Hmmm . . ." Enough small talk. Rule number 15: **Try to get the potential customer to articulate their pain without leading them in any way.** "So Brian. Let's get down to brass tacks. What do you like or not like about the bike buying process? I mean, do you find it simple and effortless, or are there some pains that accompany shopping for a bike?"

Brian thought about it as he sipped on his beer. "Well, I hate the fact that when I figure out the frame I want, I have to drive around to bike shops all over town to figure out who's carrying what."

"Oh, that's a good one. Anything else?"

"I wish there was some sort of bike rental program where I could do more that just see these new frames, but try them out for a few days. That would certainly help me make a better decision."

"Hmmm . . . that's pretty interesting." These were all great ideas, but no real problems worth solving. No migraines. Rule number 2: **Problems don't count unless they've spent time and money trying to fix them. It has to be a real need.** She decided to keep digging. "Anything about the bike buying process that was so annoying, you had to, like, go online to try to find a way to fix it? At least try to find some other people to commiserate with about it?"

"Well, I'm never sure of the right price to pay for a frame, so I'll go online to see what different stores all over the country are charging."

This sounded promising. "Tell me more about that. Do you think that's saved you a bunch of money? Like, it put you in a better negotiating position with the stores?"

"I guess. There are just so many bike shops in Chicago that I thought it would be dumb not to compare pricing."

Rule number 21: **Don't be all business. The more conversational you can be, the more they will share.** "I'm from Chicago, too!" Sam was excited. She'd even excuse the piece of brown rice sticking out of the corner of Brian's mouth, now that she knew she was talking to a fellow Chicagoan.

"Oh! Well that explains how we know each other. We've probably been to the same bike races. You do the Lake Michigan 25?"

Sam had no idea what the Lake Michigan 25 was, but she nodded. "Not for a while. Listen, so have you found any good resources to compare bike pricing at various shops?"

This inquisition continued for another 15 minutes. Sam wasn't getting anything interesting. No real migraine problems here. She and Brian traded a few Chicago stories, but Brian seemed intent on trying to figure out the race at which he and Sam had met, so she decided to bid Brian adieu.

"Hey, Brian. Thank you so much, but I've got to get dinner."

"Are you sure you don't want to get another beer? Maybe we can find some Goose Island."

"Ha. No, that's all right. Thanks, though. Hey, one question for you—is there anybody else from the Chicago cycle community here in Vegas for the tournament?" Rule number 11: **Always ask a potential customer if they know anyone else you could interview.**

Brian gave it some thought, "Now that you mention it, I've run into a couple of other riders from Chicago . . ."

Chapter 27

Recognize the Vanity Metrics to Avoid Big Losses

O wen looked at his watch—which was odd because he wasn't wearing a watch. It was an old habit from his old watch-wearing days at the consulting firm. One of those habits that reappears in certain situations—for Owen it was when he was either really nervous or really tired. Right now, it was definitely the latter. Yes, he had been nervous. Hell, he'd been stomach-churning nervous or the first eight hours of the day. There had been a lot to be nervous about.

There was the king-queen that he had while facing four-way action when he was certain he was up against an ace. Certain! But the flop had contained a queen, and he was almost sure nobody had a pair of pocket aces. That had been a big assumption. But it had held out and he'd won a ton.

Of course, he lost most of those winnings over the next hour. Damn pocket aces! Owen didn't like them. Didn't trust 'em. There's a saying in poker: the only thing more dangerous than an opponent having pocket aces is when you're holding them yourself. Actually, Owen didn't know if that was a poker saying, but it should be! It sounded good. Like something Amarillo Slim might say in a dark and hazy backroom poker game back in the '70s.

Owen had played the hand textbook. Pocket aces are not a hand to play slowly at an aggressive table. They should be played fiercely, raising as much as possible to get just one other player to call. That's the trick to pocket aces. Too much action is a death knell—if Owen checked and five players saw the flop, the chances of one of those players catching two pair or three of a kind or a straight increased dramatically. So the key is to raise enough to scare everybody away but one person, and from then on, it's pray for a dry flop, hope the opponent gets tied to his hand, and suck out as many chips as you can.

That's ideal play. Unfortunately, in the real world, ideal play rarely happens as the poker books explain it. Owen's initial bet just wasn't high enough. He got action from one too many players. Erick, a European pro with a lot of chips at his disposal, wasn't holding anything great to begin with, but his cards quickly turned into a straight that Owen's aces had no shot at competing with.

He played it smart. Owen folded his pocket aces as soon as he could tell he was behind in the hand. The problem was the amount of money it took to figure that out. He had to make sure that Erick wasn't just trying to bully him out of the way, and it took two big re-raises to make that confirmation.

Damn pocket aces. They are a lot harder to walk away from than any other hand.

That hand had been four hours ago, and Owen was still replaying it in his mind. It wasn't the fact that he lost the hand. Owen knew that it was impossible to win every hand and that the right move was to always fold as soon as you knew you were beat. It was the big bet he'd made on the turn, after he knew he was probably beat, that annoyed him. Easily his stupidest move of the tournament.

You're starting to play this game like you run ReBicycle, Owen! Snap out of it! You know the game—**spend the least amount of resources figuring out if your assumptions are right or wrong**, and live to fight another day!

Owen wished he had followed this advice at ReBicycle, but there were so many vanity metrics that kept him pumping time and money into the business, believing that he was on the right track. Believing that he was holding the best hand. ReBicycle's pocket aces were the awesome PR hits, all the visitors to the web site and the encouragement he was getting from his friends and family. At least he knew how to spot vanity metrics in poker.

This day was going late. That's why he was trying to figure out the time by looking at his watchless wrist. Owen had to go to his actual timepiece, his cell phone, to figure out the time. 8:40 P.M. With 100 or so players still left, that meant at least 15 more would need to be eliminated to get down to the 85 required to end play for the day. Yeah, there was no way they were going to finish today before midnight. That meant an hour dinner break soon and then right back to the action. Owen was putting his phone back in his pocket when he felt it buzz. A text from Sam.

"Dinner?"

Hmmm . . . did she mean to send this text to him? Probably not. She was probably trying to text someone else whose name was close to Owen's and accidentally got his number instead. Best to ignore it.

Another five minutes. Another buzz.

"You still in the tournament? Let's get dinner!"

So the text was meant for him. Why was Sam in town? Yes, that was an interesting development. But not interesting enough to justify dinner. Not after what happened last night. Owen was 99 percent sure Sam didn't decide to stay in town to try and make another move, but there was that 1 percent chance. Not worth it.

Back to reality. Focus on the table. Owen slid his phone back into his pocket, hoping the cards he was just dealt would take his mind off the texts. But no, 4 of spades and 8 of hearts is a terrible hand in any position. Owen had to fold. Another buzz.

"Owen! Answer me. I'm starving!"

He should text back. He felt bad for just ignoring her. And he did want to see her again. He missed having her around.

Owen started typing back a reply, but quickly changed his mind. This was a bad idea. He deleted his message and put the phone back in his pocket.

For the next 20 minutes he was able to put it out of his mind. Play picked up. He was exhausted, but there were still a number of hands to be played before the break. Owen got some good cards. First a pair of pocket nines to exploit and then an ace-2, which was his favorite hand to bluff, and bluff he did.

"Ladies and gentlemen, we are currently at 94 players. As the time is now 9 P.M., we will take an hour break for dinner and rest and then reconvene to play to 85. To ensure a proper chip count, please place your chips in your zip lock . . ."

Owen rubbed his eyes. It was going to be a long night. He got out his phone. Still nothing from Lisa, but he had several new texts from Sam.

"Hey, you're probably still at the tables. I'm still in town. Have just done 3 hours of interviews with cyclists."

And then, "Let me know when you are free. We need to discuss this."

The third text had been 15 minutes ago. "I'm serious as a heart attack. Will be at the pizza place on the mezzanine floor in 10."

Well, shit, Owen thought, at least he knew what he'd do with the next hour.

Chapter 28

Keep Interviewing Customers until You Find a Migraine Problem Worth Solving

t's amazing, Sam thought, how much 24 hours or less can change things. Ideas that pop into your head at night and seem perfect suddenly look completely flawed in the morning—like for some reason the brain puts makeup on our thoughts starting around 10 P.M. and then removes the makeup around 7 A.M., revealing all the scars and spots in their full glory.

Likewise, 24 hours also seems to be about the magic time it takes for the brain to calm down, to start thinking somewhat rationally again. Maybe that's how often your mind does a restart and—in computer lingo—clears out its cache. Sam couldn't remember the number of arguments she'd had with her husband, Stephen, where they'd get in a fight at night. She'd go to bed fuming mad and wake up not remembering what she was mad about. By lunchtime, she'd miss him already, and by dinner, she'd be sorry for whatever she had done to escalate things, and they would make up.

She was thinking about all that as she sipped a Sauvignon Blanc and looked over the menu of Il Trestinone. True, this meeting with Owen wouldn't lead to that kind of making up. Or at least that was highly unlikely, but it could give Sam a chance to leave on a high note instead of that little incident last night. Which is what it was—a little incident. No more overthinking it. They were two adults who had just had a little bit too much to drink. It didn't mean anything beyond that. Besides, she now had some ideas to offer up about ReBicycle, or at least observations from talking to Brian and then two of his friends.

Since when did some dough, sauce, and cheese cost 30 bucks? If there was one business she could never figure out, it was restaurants. Some seemed to charge such exorbitant prices. Others seemed to charge so little that it was amazing they stayed in business at all. Sam was exploring the $20 desserts when she saw Owen approaching over the top of the menu. Her heart jumped a little bit—just a little.

"You look like you've aged five years."

"That's what 12 hours of poker will do to you."

"Hungry?"

"Starving."

Sam flipped him the menu.

"Take a look at that. Don't worry about the prices. I've already got a tab going." She noticed Owen trying to stifle a yawn. He hadn't responded to her remark about the prices. "How's poker going? You still killing it?"

"Stupid pocket aces, Sam."

For the next 10 minutes Owen explained his day at the tables. There was definitely a lot he was glossing over and he never said whether he was still in the tournament, but she got the sense that he was still in but somewhat struggling. Best not to mention it or ask how many chips he had at this point. As a baseball fan, she knew that you never mentioned a pitcher's no-hitter, and for a poker amateur of Owen's skill level to still be in the world's biggest poker tournament, she felt the same advice applied. Best to ask general questions and let Owen fill in what he wanted.

"Any big names still at the tables?"

"Seems like there's nothing but big names left. At my table earlier in the day was Howard Lederer."

"And?"

"And he was really quiet. He moved tables after an hour because I think they wanted him where they had cameras set up or something."

"What about Phil Helmuth?"

"Yeah. He's still in, too. I've heard the crowd heckle him a couple of times. Fortunately, I haven't been near him whatsoever."

"Anybody dominating?"

"There's a guy named Greg Masters. He has nearly twice the amount of chips as the next highest chip count. He's some finance guy who's apparently a pro, but I hadn't heard of him before yesterday when he started going on a tear. Definitely the crowd favorite."

"Anybody in the crowd cheering you on yet?"

"Oh, yeah. A ton of people. They all want to see the legend that is Owen Chase and his amazingly successful bike business."

Sam laughed. Owen still did have the sarcastic edge.

"Well, cheers then."

"Cheers, Sam!"

The waiter came by. Owen was still looking at the menu, but because she knew he was pressed for time Sam just decided to order a bunch of food and they could pick what they wanted. One antipasto plate, one large margarita pizza, and two desserts. The waiter also brought a wine glass for Owen, but he pushed it to the side. Owen sighed loudly and slumped a little in his chair.

"How would you have played the aces?"

"Similar."

"No, you wouldn't. You would have folded earlier."

"Well, I would have probably checked on the turn and not made a huge bet, but that's hindsight, Owen. As an entrepreneur, you should know that sometimes you can have the best hand and not win. Lose everything. Sometimes you can have a terrible hand and still win. Everybody likes to think that because they've got their MBA or PhD or whatever, they can get rid of the luck, but luck is still a part of the game."

"So you're saying that ReBicycle could be a great idea and still fail?"

"I didn't say that." She smiled. She was impressed that Owen held out this long to bring the conversation back to ReBicycle.

"Since I've been living, breathing poker—even dreaming poker—I've been thinking a lot about poker versus business. The analogies there are really strong."

The antipasto plate came out, and Owen wasted no time in digging in. "You know what I've really learned playing poker? It's not how to bluff or when to bluff. It's when to control yourself. These pros have a ridiculous level of self-control. You can just tell. Like no pro would have kept betting those pocket aces because that's just spending good money chasing after bad. And I feel like I need that same level of self-control with ReBicycle. I haven't found a migraine problem worth solving. And I don't have the cash to convince people that buying my bikes online is safe or a good deal. So when do I pull the plug? When do I just stop throwing good money after bad?"

"I hear what you're saying, Owen. There hasn't been a lot in your customer interviews to get excited about. But the fact that your straight doesn't hit doesn't mean you can't turn your cards into a flush. I've done some interviews; you've done a lot. Is there anything here we're not seeing? Are there other migraines out there that have to do with the bike buying or owning process? There must be. This is such a huge industry."

"You tell me, Sam."

"Well, I talked to this Brian guy. He said that he tried ordering a bike online but it was a terrible experience because the shipping was so poor. Maybe that's an option. Some sort of fix to bike shipping. A new box or shipping method. You could affect a pretty large customer segment with a bike shipping solution."

Owen was reflecting on her suggestion.

"Wow, that's a totally different direction."

"Well, sure, Owen. You've done enough customer interviews to confirm your current model isn't really solving a problem. You've got a losing hand. That business model is totally flawed and you're only out is to fold. You can either fold now or waste more time and money and fold later."

"Thanks for the pep talk."

"The good news is that you still have some chips left to play. You're still in the tournament; you still have time to play a couple more hands. Maybe if you keep talking to your potential customers, you can find a real migraine problem in the bike industry. The shipping suggestion is just that. A suggestion. What else have you learned in your conversations with customers that might describe a migraine problem? Anything that stood out in your conversations? Anything that sounded like a serious problem? Even if it was totally out of left field."

Long pause. Owen closed his eyes. It was clear he was trying to think, but was having little success coming up with a good example. Sam tried a different tactic, "Okay. What about anything before Vegas—"

"Wait. There was one guy at the tables who was talking about bike shares."

"Okay, what was he saying?"

"He was a councilman or something, and I was talking with this other guy named James about bikes when he said that his city was having difficulty getting their bike share program off the ground."

"Okay. What else?"

"That was pretty much it. I asked him where they were buying their bikes and he said China. I can't compete with China."

"That's an assumption, Owen! What else did he say?"

Owen racked his brain again.

"Later in the evening, when he was talking to somebody else, he said that the repairs from China take forever."

"That's awesome. What's his name?"

"I don't know. I didn't get his name . . . wait." Owen dug into his wallet and pulled out a stack of business cards. "I think he was one of those guys here who gives everyone at the table their business card when they sit down. Yeah. It's one of these."

Sixty seconds later, they had their man. Shawn Malloy. Urban planner. City of Charlotte, North Carolina. Owen called the number on the card, but no answer.

"Try again, Owen."

He hit the redial button on his phone. "Sam. Bike share programs are a different beast altogether from building used bicycles. We're talking . . ."

She could hear someone pick up on the other end and reached over and grabbed the phone before Owen had a chance to say anything.

"Hello? Yes. I was calling for Mr. Malloy. Mr. Malloy, you gave me your business card at one of the tables here and I happened to overhear you mention something about Charlotte trying to start a bike share program . . ."

Sam adopted a slight southern drawl while talking to Shawn. He and Sam exchanged some pleasantries. She could see Owen playing with the stir-stick in his coffee, looking nervous.

"And . . ." He mimed to her. She waved him off.

"Oh yes, Mr. Malloy. I'm sorry to hear that. Had some bad beats myself. How soon? Well, yes, we'll definitely try to make that. Thank you. By 'we' I mean myself and my business partner . . . Okay, Shawn it is. Well, Shawn, I hope to see you soon."

"What's up?" Owen asked.

Sam threw a hundred on the table and she grabbed Owen's hand. "We're getting out of here. Our boy Shawn leaves town in an hour."

"I've got poker to play, Sam!"

"You've got 30 minutes!" She got up from the table and started walking toward the elevators at a brisk, morning mall walker pace. She turned to see Owen still at the table deciding on what to do.

"Come on, Owen!" She motioned with her arm.

He got up from the table, smiled, and threw his napkin down.

Chapter 29

People Can't Help Themselves from Sharing When You Bring Up a Migraine Problem

I t had taken Owen a week, but he'd finally figured Sam out. Yes, she may have been a successful entrepreneur. Yes, she was wicked smart. Yes, she was fun. But more than all of that, she was rich and bored. And if there was anything Owen had learned from hanging around the consulting firm, it was that bored, rich people loooooooove to solve other people's problems because they don't have any real problems of their own.

Owen remembered his former boss for this eccentricity. His biggest problem was keeping his affair with the aerobics instructor at his club away from his wife. Not an unsolvable problem, in Owen's opinion, because he could have called it off at any moment. And even though his boss was pretty obviously unsatisfied with marriage and relationships and whatever, that didn't stop him from trying to be Owen's dating coach.

After a year of working at the consulting firm, Owen finally learned that when he wanted to leave work early, all he had to do was go tell the boss that he was going to pop out of the office early to get ready for a date. Without fail, the boss would want to know every detail about the girl and the date. How many times had Owen used that excuse before he met Lisa? Probably once a month, minimum. In fact, he hesitated to say anything about Lisa around the office for some time because it meant he had to come up with new excuses to leave work at 4:30 P.M. The boss wasn't as interested in long-term relationships as he was in bachelorhood. Go figure.

Owen was thinking about all of that as he tried to keep up with Sam. She was very much like his old boss. But instead of being interested in his dating life (well, she did seem slightly interested in that), she was interested in his business, interested in helping "fix it," just like his boss had been interested in "fixing" his love life. He shook his head and wondered where the heck they were going. Sam hadn't told him. She was kidnapping him, for all he knew. Finally, they got into a taxi and Sam ordered it to go to Caesar's Palace. Owen checked his phone for the time. The players would be getting back to the tables in about 25 minutes to start the next level of the WSOP. Whatever this rabbit hole was, he hoped that it was going to be worth it.

Sam turned to him in the cab, "So you'll be able to spot the guy?"

"What?"

"The guy. Shawn Mallory. "

"It's Malloy, and yeah, I'll remember him." Owen didn't remember at all what he looked like, but how hard could it be? "Why are we in such a hurry, Sam?"

"We're meeting him in a restaurant. He said he's at the bar finishing up dinner and getting ready to catch a ride with a friend to the airport. That's why we're rushing."

"Well, at least he's on a time crunch, too." Hopefully, they could have a quick chat and Owen wouldn't have to miss any poker.

The taxi dropped them off at Caesar's, and Sam practically bumrushed the door to get in the casino. Owen was afraid he was going to lose her in the crowd.

"Okay, Owen, where is he?"

"He's . . ." Owen scanned the room, but didn't see anybody that looked familiar. He then realized he had this guy's number on his phone and was trying to get to the recent-calls screen when he felt someone slap his shoulder.

"Hey, man! I just saw the odds. Didn't know you were still in the tourney. Congratulations, Owen. What kind of bike you gonna get after this run?"

It was Shawn all right. The wide smile, general happiness, and slap on the back were all hallmarks of overly friendly casino floor managers and low-level politicians—and the Southern drawl gave Shawn away.

"Hey, Shawn. Yep. It's ridiculous. What do you mean my odds?"

"At the Sportsbook here. Now that there are under 100 players, you can bet on who you think will win the World Series."

"And I'm on there?"

"You were . . . unless you were knocked out since I last checked?" That thought made Shawn frown in an overly dramatic way.

"No. I'm still in. I'm just here for a few minutes because . . . well, this is my friend Sam and we want to know more about your bike share program."

Shawn swiveled around and clapped his hands together. "Why . . . how rude of me not to notice you. Forgive me." He took Sam's hand and delicately held it up. "Sam, the pleasure is all mine. And may it be too presumptuous of me to assume Sam is short for Samantha?"

Owen had never seen *Gone with the Wind*, but if he had to guess how all the gentleman behaved in the movie, it would be a lot like

Shawn laying down the Southern charm. Shawn had even gotten Sam to blush a little.

"Not presumptuous at all, Shawn. Do you want to get a seat?"

"I already acquired a table for us after we got off the phone. This way."

As they were walking to Shawn's table, he kept asking Owen about the tournament and various players. It seemed Shawn knew more than Owen did about what was going on. Owen wasn't too surprised to learn that Greg Masters was the favorite to win it right now. He was kind of disappointed to find out that he was bunched in with several other amateurs in the 50-to-1 odds. Disappointed, but not really surprised. There were already drinks for Shawn and Sam at the table.

"Now, Sam, if you're looking for an expert in bicycles, let me tell you that you've got yourself a great resource. I played with Mr. Chase here for a good portion of yesterday, and he is quite the whiz on all things related to cycling."

"Actually, Shawn, we're here because of Owen." Sam nodded at Owen, which apparently was supposed to be his cue to start asking Shawn questions. He was still a little confused about how exactly Shawn worked with bikes, so he decided to start there.

"Shawn, you're in charge of the bike sharing program in Charlotte, right?"

"Well . . . in charge is not the right word. We actually don't have a person in charge, which is part of the problem we're having—the city budgeted the money for these bikes and the program, but they didn't budget any for staff to run the program. I've kind of unofficially taken up the mantle since I was involved with our first orders of bikes a couple of months ago."

"And how did that go?" Sam leaned in like she was a prosecutor and Shawn was on the witness stand. Shawn didn't seem to mind. Or notice. He took a long drink of his white-whatever liquor.

"Well, to be honest, it went terribly. We'd looked, of course, at buying local, even just American, but the cost was too much . . . so then I was tasked with tracking down some factories overseas. But the city didn't want to send me overseas, so I had to try and work these deals over the phone and by e-mail, which, as you might imagine, was a little difficult with the language thing and all. And then I'd ask for samples of the bikes I wanted and the samples would take forever to ship. And trying to get the warranty figured out with these companies. . . ." He rolled his eyes. "Frankly, it's been more trouble than it's worth. I mean, the program hasn't even officially launched in the city and we're running into all these supplier issues already."

Now Owen's interest was piqued. "What did you do to try to solve this problem?"

"Well, I go to a conference every year for city planners, urban developers, councilmen, and the like. You know, people from all over the country gather together, and we talk about our issues and listen to presentations. Well, it's funny that you're asking me about this because that conference just wrapped up for this year in Seattle. I spent the week there before I came to Vegas, and there was a symposium on bike sharing programs, and it sure seemed like we weren't the only city dealing with this problem."

"Every city?!" Owen was excited.

"Uh, let's see. Santa Fe, San Antonio, St. Louis, Calgary in Canada. There were some others."

"And they've all had issues getting bikes for their bike share programs?"

"Either that or they've just given up because it's a nightmare right now. The big-time companies don't want to play with us because we can't pay enough per unit and the small-time foreign companies are delivering junk."

"And how much are you guys looking to spend per unit?"

"Around $1,500 plus another $200 for warranty and repair."

Owen didn't have a glass of water to spit out or he would have. That was more than he was charging! More than twice his prices! His toes were tapping.

"So have you considered used bikes?"

"Not really. These are specialty-designed bikes. They have to weigh a certain amount so they don't get stolen, they need to have certain computer parts, and we need the bikes to be like a fleet. All built relatively the same, look the same. I don't have time to be putting together a used fleet piecemeal."

Well, at least Owen understood the higher price tag per bike. He wasn't sure what computer parts Shawn was talking about, but how hard could it be to figure out? They couldn't possibly cost more than half the value of the bike.

"So, what if there was a company that did just that? They took used parts and built new bikes out of them, repainted them. Sold them in that $1,500 price range and included a warranty. Is that something you might consider?"

"Well, of course. But I don't think anything like that exists."

"I want to kiss you, Shawn."

"Well . . . uh, thank you, Owen." Now it was Shawn's turn to blush.

"Well, then . . . I think we all need a drink," Sam said.

Chapter 30

Stay Objective in Your Interviews Whether You Are Getting Good or Bad News

"Yes, it was interesting, Owen."

"Well, we'll see, Owen."

"That's an assumption, Owen."

Sam was deflecting Owen's rapid-fire questions and couldn't help but think how funny it all was. She had to basically interrogate Owen into remembering the bike share thing, and once she did, she literally had to drag him to meet with Shawn.

And now look at him. She had to practically pry Owen away from the conversation with Shawn so that he wouldn't miss any more poker, and now, in the taxi, his mind seemed to be going a million miles an hour—with none of his thoughts focusing on poker. After a moment, Sam shrugged. Falling in love with an idea is like falling in love with a person—you can't just talk someone out of it. You have to let them see the light themselves, and it was clear that Owen was already getting ahead of himself now that bike share programs around the country might be a possibility. But she had to let him enjoy it a little. It's not often that someone gets a taste of a possible migraine problem worth solving.

Possible being the operative word. *Possible migraine problem.*

"So this is definitely a problem worth solving, right, Sam? You agree this is in the migraine category?"

"It might be, Owen."

"What do you mean might? You're being too negative."

"I'm not being anything besides rational. You just had one conversation. That's it. One. That's like playing one hand of poker and getting pocket aces and expecting all your hands to be pocket aces."

Owen rolled his eyes. "It was clearly a big problem, Sam. I've proven that there are customers who want my product."

"Whoa. First, I told you that finding a problem worth solving is only half of the equation. And what if this is like my sister's breast pump? What if this is a one-off migraine?"

"But Shawn said he just got back from the conference and everybody was having the issue."

"It was one conference, and he was talking with people he doesn't know that well. I used to go to tech conferences all the time and would agree with people just to get them to stop talking."

"So what's your take, Sam?"

Sam looked out the window. She couldn't shake something about Mr. Shawn Malloy. He definitely had some huckster in his blood. What part was Shawn feeling actual pain in his urban planning job and what part was Shawn agreeing with Owen because he could guess what Owen wanted to hear? Or because as long as he was agreeing, he was enjoying the attention of a pretty girl?

"You gonna answer, Sam?"

"It's . . . it's promising, but there's still a ton left to do. After all, the normal city urban planner whatever guy in every city doesn't also play in the World Series of Poker, so Shawn Malloy is definitely an outlier in many ways. But if what he's saying is true for some other bike share programs, then there could be something here."

The taxi arrived back at the Rio. Sam turned and faced Owen. It wasn't in a sexy I-wanna-kiss way. At least Sam hoped that's not what she was conveying. She was trying to look as serious as possible, to reinforce her next words. They'd mean life or death for ReBicycle.

"Owen . . . look at me. You have to start your assumptions and validations from scratch. All new assumptions. All new customer interviews. I know it's difficult to say screw it to all the work you've done interviewing so far, but that's what you have to do. From scratch, okay?"

"From scratch. Got it." He finally acquiesced.

"And even if you find customers with a problem worth solving, you'll still need to prove that they will actually buy your product. That your product solves their problem. All these interviews you've been doing are just half of the equation."

"Thanks, Sam." Owen looked like he was going in for a hug but then stopped himself.

"Want me to come cheer you on at the tables?"

He looked uncomfortable. He wasn't answering. He might be taking this the wrong way. Sam reflected on which way she actually meant it. It just sort of came out. She wasn't really thinking things through. She just didn't want to go back to her lonely hotel room and watch more bad TV.

"I'm sure you've got lots of people in Vegas who want to see you," he said. "You don't have to feel the need to keep me company. I'm just going to go in the zone for the next few hours, you know?"

And she made it awkward again. In a way, she felt bad about making him feel uncomfortable about the situation, but somewhere deep down, her competitive drive came alive. Who is this guy to be so uninterested in Sam Donovan? She wasn't used to that kind of treatment.

"I've got to run, Sam. I'm late." And with that Owen ran out of the cab. Didn't even offer to pay the fare.

Sam walked what oddly felt like a walk of shame into the hotel by herself. She stopped just short of the entry doors to enjoy the desert air for a moment. On past trips to Vegas, she'd be dying to leave after a week on the Strip. But this time, it almost felt too soon. She'd relish her last day in Sin City tomorrow. Who knew what it would bring?

Chapter 31

Nothing Else Matters until You Can Prove That Customers Want Your Product

Three A.M. That's what? 5 A.M. central. And 6 A.M. in Columbus. People would be getting up soon to go to work. Keep working, Owen.

Owen looked down at the notepad of hotel stationery that contained his assumption scribbles. True, the writing wasn't the best, but that's what happens when you try and use a pencil with a feather-top pillow as a backstop. He could still make out the chicken scratch that was his initial set of assumptions:

Customer: Bike share programs.

Problem: Their ability to get quality fleet bicycles at affordable prices.

That was pretty specific. Owen couldn't believe how far he had come in such a short amount of time. The old Owen in his position would have worried whether the name ReBicycle would need to be changed for the new customer segment. He would have done a sketch drawing of how the web site would need to change to provide the maximum value. He would have gone online to look for potential sales reps that could market to bike share programs all over the country.

But the new Owen knew that none of that work would mean a lick if his original assumptions about the customer and problem weren't right. The new Owen understood that **nothing else matters until you can prove that customers want your product**. He'd been down the other road before, and this time, he would save himself a lot of time, money, and emotional energy by focusing on the main thing that mattered: Was he solving a problem for a specific group of customers? Did he understand who customers 1 through 10 would be? How he would find them? What migraine was he addressing for them?

Owen was too excited about the possibility that he was on to something. He saw the pupils dilate in Shawn's eyes when he talked about the difficulty of buying bicycle fleets. There was something here.

Owen thought about the surreal nature of his entire time in Vegas. Just tonight, as he was getting up from the poker table at 12:30 A.M., happy with a chip stack of $900,000 (not a large amount of chips for the room, but enough to get him through the day), he heard a small crowd cheering for him as he walked out of the poker room. Whatever adrenaline had died down at the close of the day returned as soon as he heard the hollers from the crowd. He had fans! What a weird world. Seven days ago, close friends weren't even returning phone calls because they didn't want to hear about ReBicycle, and now complete strangers were shaking his hand and telling him he was their favorite player in the tournament.

He was trying not to let all of it go to his head. And he wasn't sure whether he was more excited about the poker success or the fact that he might have stumbled on a migraine problem worth solving. He needed help testing these assumptions. He wouldn't have time to make the calls he needed to on his own tomorrow.

He reached for his phone. Still nothing from Lisa. She had e-mailed him earlier in the day telling him she was fine, but no other communication. He would deal with it when he got home. Nothing he could do from Vegas other than sending her another apology e-mail and begging her to come spend some time with him here.

He dialed Stephanie, head of the ReBicycle marketing team.

"Hello?"

"Hey, Stephanie . . . you awake?"

"Uh, sure, Owen. Is everything okay?"

"Things are great. I've survived another day of poker and am still in the tournament."

"Yeah, we've been following you online. Plus, the most popular Google search to ReBicycle's web site over the past two days has been people who have been looking up your name, so you've got to be doing something right."

Owen laughed. "Yeah. That's pretty much the gist of it. Listen, Stephanie, I think I may have discovered a new need for our products. But so far, I just have a gut feeling from a single conversation. This need is just an assumption at this point. And I need your help running an experiment to prove it true or false. Does that make sense?"

Stephanie seemed confused. Owen was speaking in a whole new foreign language. He tried explaining to her the importance of finding a migraine problem worth solving, and proving the value of ReBicycle to a specific customer group. Stephanie was quiet on the line. She was just taking it all in.

"So I'd like you to find the numbers for as many bike share programs in the country as you can."

"Bike shares?"

"Yeah, they are programs where you can rent a bike for an hour or for the day. Just search for them online; you'll find a bunch. I need you to call those programs and talk to their executive director or whoever is in charge about how they source their bicycles."

"Okay."

"Do you have a pen handy? I have specific questions I need you to ask."

Owen explained the important questions:

How do you currently get your bikes for the bike lending program?
Are you happy with this solution?
What other options have you considered/tried? And why did you not choose them?
How much are you spending on your bikes now? How many bikes per year?

He felt that these questions would be the most nonleading questions that would provide him with the greatest amount of insight.

"Remember, we aren't trying to sell them anything."

"I don't even know that we have anything to sell them, Owen."

"I'm just saying, your goal is to listen on these calls and to see if you can pick up a real problem worth solving. Probe their answers for further information. The deeper the answers you can get to these questions, the easier it will be for us to prove this assumption true or false."

"What is this, Owen?"

"Please, just trust me. It's getting late here and this is important. Please let me know at the end of the day how these calls went. I want the whole marketing team on this. As many calls as you can make."

Chapter 32

Luck Makers Seek Out New Experiences and Find Opportunities Wherever They Go

"A wake?"

Five minutes later.

"Got a lot of good ideas. Wanna run some by you."

Two minutes later.

"Oh btw . . . I'm still in the tourney."

Those were the three messages from Owen that Sam discovered on her cell phone when she awoke. That was good. Sam knew

Owen and human nature enough to know that if there had been no messages from him, that would have meant he was out of the tournament. The fact that there were three messages must mean that he was still in a pretty decent position. Or maybe he was just surviving. Who knew? She'd go see him play today. It was a big day. Eighty-five players were going to be narrowed down to just 27. Only three tables of players would be left standing by the end of the day. It was incredibly unlikely that Owen was going to make it that far, so she could be there to make him feel better once he got knocked out.

"Awesome! You're gonna hear me cheer today!"

She immediately regretted the text as soon as she hit send. That was a little too chipper. Too optimistic. Too something.

There was no end time given for today's round of play—just a start time of 11, an hour break for lunch at 3 P.M. and a dinner break at 10 P.M., with a few shorter breaks in between. Sam thought about how Owen could end up playing another 12-plus hours of poker today and shuddered. Frankly, she'd been angry that she'd been eliminated as early as she was and in the way she was, but she hadn't missed the play at all.

The idea of watching 12 hours of poker—much less playing in it—was enough to make her anxious. Oh, well, the likelihood of his making it all day was incredibly low.

Sam got on her computer and checked the details of her flight. Still on time and scheduled to leave at 7 P.M. That actually fit perfect with the World Series of Poker schedule. She could eat and talk with Owen one last time, if he made it to the 3 P.M. break, and then leave the hotel around 4:30 P.M. and be at the airport in plenty of time to catch her flight this time.

Sam drank the last of the pot of coffee in her room and switched into some running shorts and a tank top. She checked her watch—10 A.M. on the dot. One hour was plenty of time to get in a run, grab some breakfast, and still clean up to watch Owen. Hell, maybe she'd see Owen working out this morning. They did seem to have a thing about running into each other in the gym. For a moment, she considered texting him again to ask him if he wanted to meet there, but then decided against it. The last text from him came at nearly 4 A.M. He was probably still sleeping.

Surprisingly, even though the hotel had already started to clear out a little, the gym was still packed. Even more so than the first couple days of the tournament. And it seemed like Sam recognized every other person. True, poker players are by nature a sedentary bunch, but most of the pros were very strict about their workout schedules.

Owen wasn't there. Someone who may or may not have been Phil Ivey was riding an exercise bike while flipping through a finance magazine. The treadmills were relatively untouched and Sam took what had become her favorite—the one closest to the entrance where she could not only see who was coming in but also see the rest of the gym through the wall mirrors.

Eighteen minutes and nearly 2.5 miles later Sam was definitely feeling the heavy Italian pizza and wine from the night before. Work through it, Sam! She tried changing the songs on her playlist but nothing motivating came on. Television was a mix of boring day-time programs. Damn . . . there was just nothing to fire her up. Fine. At least get to the 20-minute mark and then you can stop. It'd be short of her goal of a 5K (3.1 miles) in 22 minutes, but it was better than nothing.

Almost instantly, Sam's plans changed as she saw Greg Masters walk through the door. Sam knew, as did everyone in the hotel and Vegas, that Masters was not just leading the WSOP but leading it by a huge margin. He had been at the top of the leader board since day three or four and now his lead seemed untouchable.

It was also Sam's first time sizing him up close. It was definitely him—he was a dead ringer for the photo she saw online. But from what she had heard from Owen and others, she was expecting him to be shorter and less fit. But no, he was pretty tall and pretty svelte. Though the goatee . . . she wasn't sure about the goatee. What really drew Sam in was his face. It was such an unassuming face, but one that she was sure she'd seen somewhere before. Masters flashed a smile at Sam and got on a treadmill next to hers. Whatever motivation she'd been looking for, she just found it. Bump up the speed a little and take it to the full 5K!

Actually, 5K turned into nearly 7K and 30 minutes. The last five minutes of which had been difficult—very difficult. She was drenched in sweat. And for what? To impress Greg Masters? To prove she could run with him? She wasn't sure why she had run the extra minutes, but it had something to do with Greg's presence.

Wiping down the machine. A quick glance at Masters. Him focused straight ahead on whatever the television on his treadmill was showing. Not paying attention . . .

"Hey."

Greg had taken out his left ear-bud and looked at Sam while running. It was only then that Sam realized she'd been staring in Master's general direction. She quickly continued scrubbing down her treadmill.

"Hey (huff), I know you (huff huff); you gave a speech at a conference (huff) about angel investing (huff). Sparksys right? (Huff) What's your name?"

"Sam."

"Nice to meet you again, Sam (huff). It was a good speech (huff). Damn good speech (huff). I'm (huff, huff) Greg."

She smiled.

"I know you. Good luck in the tournament."

"You in?"

Sam was impressed that Masters was attempting conversation while running, especially considering he'd just ramped up the speed past 8.5. If he was struggling to run and talk at the same time, he wasn't really showing it. His breathing was heavy but constant. He was a natural runner. There must have been some cross-country in his younger days. Who knows, maybe even cycling. But for right now, she'd let the question go on too long.

"No. I'm here because my flight got canceled and I'm cheering on a friend."

"What's the friend's name?"

"Owen Chase."

Pause. Masters was replaying the name in his head.

"Don't know him."

"He's the guy with the messed up leg."

"Ohhhh. (Huff) Biker-Boy.

"That's him."

"You know, he was at my table."

"I did not know that." Sam couldn't believe Owen hadn't told her he was at the table with the chip leader. No wonder he seemed so stressed at the beginning of dinner. "Well, take it easy on him."

Greg Masters laughed. He started slowing down the treadmill and didn't say anything for almost 30 seconds. Finally he pushed the "cool down" button. Sam was still wiping down her treadmill; she didn't even know why anymore.

'Well . . . tell Biker-Boy I say hello."

"You'll see me cheering him on today."

"We'll see for how long," he said with a grin.

And like that, Masters left the gym. No formal good-bye. Just a smile. Sam didn't know where Masters was from, but she liked his abrupt style. She looked again at the time. She'd been on the treadmill for 10 minutes too long. She'd have to decide between breakfast, shower, and showing up late.

She decided on a shower and getting a good seat. Breakfast could wait. Owen needed her cheering, especially with a guy like Greg Masters at the table.

Chapter 33

Luck Is Not a Good Strategy for Poker or Business—It's the Outcome of a Good Strategy

O wen yawned and looked at his phone again. He told himself he didn't really care if Sam saw him play poker or not. Yes, it would be nice, but there had been players who practically had entire cheering sections, and it didn't seem to help. He wasn't superstitious in that way. In fact, his performance would probably be better without her or anyone he knew around . . . fewer distractions.

Except for Lisa. He'd love to have her in the crowd. Just to know that she was okay. That she wasn't out meeting with a lawyer, arranging for divorce papers. Put that out of your mind, Owen. She's just mad. You can fix this when you get home. If you can find a way to potentially fix ReBicycle, then you can fix this thing with Lisa . . . whatever it is.

Back to the poker. At this point in the tournament, every table became a "featured" table, meaning that they were set up for audio, lights, pinhole cameras that could see the cards, and big stationary cameras with bored-looking cameramen at several different vantage points around the table. It added another little sense of pressure. And it also meant that cell phones were now banned at the tables. Phone calls were not allowed before, but texting and e-mail had been okay.

The new cell phone rule had a couple of implications. To answer a text from Lisa or Sam or Pitchford or whoever, Owen would have to physically get up from the table, move at least 30 feet away from the floor and still try to observe play to make sure he didn't miss his next hand. He knew he couldn't afford to miss a good hand. It might mean the difference between going out in the morning and actually making a run to the final 27 players.

It was a high-class problem. Today was a new day. A new table. Four of the players at Owen's table had already arrived. He recognized a couple of them. Fortunately, no famous pros yet. Owen looked at his phone again—out of habit more than anything. Only five minutes until play began. Suddenly, Owen could hear several large Ziploc bags of chips making their way to his table.

"Morning."

Shit! Owen instantly knew he'd drawn Greg Masters at his table again. This was not the bit of luck he'd been hoping for today. Greg was still laying all of his chips out on the table when play started. After a few moments, somebody with an ESPN shirt came by and hooked up Masters to his very own mic, which Owen couldn't figure out—there were already boom mikes above the table, and it wasn't like Masters even talked while he played. The only humorous part of the morning had been when the last three players to the table showed up smiling, scanned the table, saw Masters, and immediately dropped their smiles. "I feel like a gladiator in the Coliseum," Owen heard one of them mutter.

Whatever it was about having the mic on him, it seemed to open Masters up, *open up* being a relative term, meaning Masters said a couple of words every half-hour. Owen had also kept pretty quiet for the first few hours. There had been a conversation about *Cops* and *48 Hours* and reality crime shows, and Owen had participated a little. But other than that, he just focused on the cards and thought about what results Stephanie was going to be able to have by the end of the day.

"So what happened to your leg?"

It was Masters. He'd been on a bit of a dry streak and Owen noticed he was more talkative during the dry spells than the winning spells.

"I injured it in a bike accident."

"Like motorcycle or bicycle?"

"Bicycle."

"Oh, are you Biker-Boy?"

Owen laughed. So it was true, he had a nickname. A couple of players had called him Biker-Boy after he started asking questions, but he didn't think it had caught on. But if Masters knew it, it must have spread. This was not such a bad thing.

"Yeah, I guess so."

"Cool."

Masters nodded his head. Conversation done. But still, he'd engaged Owen and wasn't giving him the death stare. So far, so good.

Another hour. Another relatively dry run of play. And one more elimination. An old grizzled pro Owen had never heard of had a small stack and got a player with a really, really, small stack to go all-in. The grizzled pro won, and just like that, the table was down to seven people. Instead of new people filling in the seats of those eliminated, like they had done throughout the tournament so far, these seats remained empty. The floor boss said that after the 3 P.M. hiatus, they'd reorganize and break up the smallest tables.

Considering there were some tables with only five or six people left, there was a good chance Owen was stuck at this table for a while.

Finally, right before the 3 P.M. break, play picked up for Owen. Ace-2, a couple of suited connectors in a row, and then in late position he looked down at this hand to see his old favorite ace-king. The only other player was Masters, who had gone in for a small raise—nothing out of the ordinary there. For a second, Owen thought about just calling, but this late in the tournament against a player like Masters, he had to show strength through a raise.

"100 grand."

That got the table's attention. Masters raised an eyebrow but didn't say anything. Both the big and small blind folded. It was up to Masters. He looked at his cards one more time. Played with some of his chips. He took a deep breath and played with his chips some more. Then boom. A call.

That was when the sweat started. Owen had done his best to avoid Masters, to stay in his good graces. Hell, he and Masters had even had a conversation. But now that was all gone. Owen looked at his cards again. Ace-king. He had folded it once this tournament, but unless the flop was terrible, it'd be really hard to fold it a second time.

The dealer was also new for the day, apparently chosen for her dramatic, camera-ready, dealing style, and she took her sweet time turning the flop, ratcheting up the tension. Finally, though, Owen was looking at an ace and 3-3. He flopped high pair plus the 3-3 gave him a shot at a full house. Whatever Masters did, Owen already knew what his next play would be.

"850,000 to Biker-Boy," Masters said.

Whoa! He had not been expecting Masters to make that big a bet; $850,000 was the amount of chips Owen had left—Masters was daring him to call all-in. And . . . and he had said something. Masters almost never said anything when making a bet. One more look at his ace-king. The two hands that could beat Owen were if Masters had pocket aces or a 3. If he had an ace-3, Owen was really in trouble, but it was tough to tell. Masters was again hiding behind his chips. Owen took a minute to consider the $100,000 he had already committed to the pot. If he folded now, then he'd still have a decent amount left. His stack would be on the small side, but not the lowest in the tournament. If he went all-in and won, well, then he'd have nearly $2 million. . . . Owen played with his chips as he gave it more thought.

"Dealers, please finish all current hands and do not deal again until you are told to do so. We will begin our one-hour afternoon break in approximately five minutes. Thank you."

So now the emcee had added to the pressure. Last hand of morning play. Fold or . . . oh, screw it. Folding here is idiotic. Go for it!

"ALL-IN!"

He said it forcefully. With power! He didn't even bother to push his chips in. That was his little sign to the audience. He'd learned over the past week that players called all-in without pushing in their chips when they were absolutely sure of their win. Owen just flipped his ace-king over and stared at Masters. He didn't even want to look at Masters's cards—just stare down the man himself as if that could possibly change the outcome of the all-in call.

"Hey. Why you keep staring at me, Biker-Boy?" Masters was smiling. Only then did Owen look down at Masters's hand and see that he was holding an Ace-three. Owen held his breath. He instantly felt his head get warm and start deploying beads of sweat in an effort to cool itself. He was in big trouble. He was about to get knocked out of the tournament.

Owen put his head down at the table; he didn't want to see the next card come out. He wanted to take it back. He wanted a do-over. He heard the dealer pound the table twice with her hand, as they typically did before discarding a card face down and laying down the next card, the turn. He heard loud cheers and wasn't sure what they meant.

Owen looked up to see that the turn card was a king of clubs. He was still alive. But his chances were on life support. In order to make it through this hand, Owen would have to suck out one of the only two remaining kings in the deck. He was hopeful, but he knew his odds were not good. Owen put his head down again. Maybe that would work again this time. It seemed to bring him some luck before.

As he closed his eyes, he cursed the predicament he had gotten himself into. He had mediocre cards and was now putting his whole tournament life in jeopardy. He had to get lucky now. He had made a huge mistake. He knew that. Owen vowed that he would not only play better poker from now on, but he would not put his new business opportunity in the same situation. He would wait until he had the best hand this time around. He would make sure ReBicycle didn't need to depend on luck this time around.

Owen felt someone pat him on the back. One of the other players at the table. He didn't even look up to see who it was. He was so scared and just felt like a fool. Greg Masters had played him perfectly. Owen was replaying the call over and over in his mind when he felt another double knock on the table, and then . . .

More cheering, even louder cheering. He looked up to see another king on the board. He won! He looked at Greg Masters for confirmation, and Greg was smiling and shaking his head.

"Congratulations, Biker-Boy. Just know I'm coming back to get my chips from you after the break."

Owen took what felt like his first breath in a few minutes. Wow. He'd just survived an all-in versus Masters. Not only that, but he was up to two million chips. Owen laughed. What a ridiculous hand. What a game—oomph! Somebody was hugging him.

"Look at you!"

He recognized Sam's voice.

"Hey, Sam."

"Did you hear me yelling back there? I had all my fingers and toes crossed."

"I didn't . . . I couldn't hear anything. Were you really yelling?"

"Heck yeah. I was yelling at Masters to call all-in and knock you out!"

A laugh. And not just any laugh—a laugh that relieved a lot of tension. Owen was ready for his break. Ready to check his e-mails and see if there was anything from Lisa, or maybe Stephanie had an early progress report. He was just ready to get out of this card hall and have a nice meal with an old friend.

"Come on. Let's get out of here and grab lunch before I have to get back to the tables."

Chapter 34

To Prove Demand, Find the Shortest Path to the Ultimate Customer Action

"So wait. You outsourced these interviews?"

"I haven't outsourced anything, Sam. I told Stephanie the overall idea of what I was looking for, and then I sent her some specific questions to ask. We talked a long time. She's the heart of the ReBicycle brand. She cares that we're successful just as much as I do."

"Okay, outsourcing is a bad word. But Stephanie isn't the founder of the company. You are. Rule number 9 of customer interviews, Owen: **The founder of the company should be the one making the calls, doing the research. Otherwise it's meaningless**." Owen put another olive in his mouth. Sam sure liked things done her way.

"It's got to be the founder asking these questions. It's not that I don't think Stephanie is as smart as you or isn't part of the team. But your staff wants to get you the answers you are looking for, and they certainly don't want to deliver bad news. Best-case scenario is that she inadvertently messes with the results by leading the interviews into one direction or another. At worst, she won't tell you the truth about the calls. And she isn't as invested as you, Owen. She might be listening to answers on a superficial level instead of probing deeper and trying to discover true problems. Only the person that's going to be making decisions about the life and death of this company should be conducting these interviews."

"So what do you want me to do?" She had a point, and Owen didn't want to spend the entire lunch bickering back and forth.

"I want you to make these calls, Owen. The goal of the exercise is not for someone to get just any answers to these questions, it's for you to hear the answers and be able to make decisions. If you hadn't heard those bike store customers talk about how price wasn't a big issue yourself, you never would have admitted that the original idea was flawed. **You'll just be a lot more likely to act on this information if you gather it yourself**."

"Okay, okay. I'll make the calls." He knew she wouldn't stop until he relented. And it made sense to him. He definitely wouldn't have believed Stephanie if she had done the initial research and told him bike store shoppers didn't care about price.

"Good. Now I'm feeling more and more confident about your new venture." She lifted up her glass in his honor.

Owen clinked his glass with hers. He did feel like he was finally making progress for the first time in a year. "So then what?"

"What do you mean?"

"Well, say I prove that these bike shares have a real migraine problem."

"By making the calls yourself." She pointed at him with her glass.

"By making the calls myself, Sam. Say I figure that out. What's next? You said that finding a problem worth solving was only half of the equation. So can we spend some time talking about the second half?"

"Right! Thanks for bringing it up. Once you prove there's a migraine problem out there, you still need to prove that customers want your solution. It's not just assumed. For instance, even if price had been an issue for your customers—a huge issue for them—ReBicycle still would probably have failed because your solution was an online platform, and we learned from talking to people that they aren't really comfortable buying bicycles online. So **just finding a problem worth solving alone won't guarantee success—you have to prove that customers want your solution.**"

"And how would you like for me to prove that?"

"Every business has a specific action it wants from its customers. Remember the journey you took with the ReBicycle 1.0. You came up with an idea and you did all this stuff. You built the web site, created test bikes, made marketing materials, went after PR, hired salespeople, bought schwag, wrote a blog . . . all this stuff."

"Okay."

"But at the end of the day, all of this stuff was created to elicit a very specific action from your customers. For ReBicycle, you wanted them to buy something. Some other company might want users to sign up and use its product in some way or make a referral or whatever. So our **goal is to find the shortest path from your idea to this ultimate customer action.**"

"Okay. But I think we did that already when we were talking to Shawn and I asked him if he would buy these bikes from us if he was happy with the quality."

"Ehhh." She made a loud buzzer sound. **"Rule number 7, Owen: Never ask 'would you?' It's the worst question you could ask because you won't learn anything.** First, it's leading. Second, people will lie to you. By the time you are pitching your solution and they know what you are looking for, they will tell you that something sounds great, just so they won't hurt your feelings. **The**

only way to tell if they want it, that it actually relieves their migraine, is to get them to actually perform the ultimate action. They need to give you money, or some kind of currency."

"So, you want me to create some bike share bikes and try to sell them? Or redesign our web site to say that this is our new line of business?"

"That's probably too much work, Owen. You want to **find the shortest path possible to the ultimate action. What's the smallest bet you could make, in terms of time and money, to get your customers to give you a preorder or their credit card number, or a letter of intent or something?** It can be a sketch, a PowerPoint. Literally, your goal should be the least amount of time and money spent on creating something that can simulate the behavior you will eventually seek in your customers."

"Seriously?"

She smiled. "Yes! Seriously. You want to prove they want it, don't you? Before you spend another year and hundreds of thousands of dollars going in the wrong direction?"

Owen was skeptical. "And you think people will pay me money without having the actual bikes?"

"Yes! That's the modern age in which we live! If they really have a migraine problem and *if!*, if they think your product actually solves that problem, or they believe it might. If that's the case, they'll be hungry to try whatever it is you are selling. You should have seen me trying to sell Flybaby products to people at the airport out of a large duffle bag. I would seriously just go around and ask people with babies if there were any baby items they needed right then."

"You're joking."

"No! I told them I was trying out a new business concept and I wanted to see if they would actually buy anything. Did I get some weird looks? Sure. Did I get lectured by security a few times for trying to sell things at the airport? Once or twice. But did I get people to hand me their credit card in exchange for some baby products I carried in my duffle? Yes! That's how I knew it was going to work. Imagine spending hundreds of thousands of dollars on the infrastructure and the equipment you would need to set up the vending machines. I couldn't imagine spending that kind of time or money without first having proof that people were going to buy."

"It's that easy, huh?"

"That's the fun part, Owen. If you can get people to buy something without building it and branding it, you'll know you have something. You'll know you have the beginning of a real, sustainable, scalable company! Like if you were creating a software product, you could just create a landing page that described some core benefits and see how many people you can get to download the product or give you their credit card. You don't need to have a single line of code written. Or with ReBicycle, you don't actually need to build any bikes to get an order placed. You can probably just sell it with a phone call or a pamphlet."

She never ceased to surprise him. This was definitely a different approach. But it oddly made sense. Especially after the initial interviews trying to diagnose a problem. Sam definitely knew what she was talking about.

"You excited to try it?"

"Definitely easier said than done, Sam. I thought sales were hard when I had actual bikes to sell."

She raised her glass again.

"Easier with all the poker money you're about to get. You know you're quite a celebrity in this town now. I'm glad I invested in you when your personal stock was still affordable. Now, just as I'm leaving town, you're becoming this big deal."

"Yep. You're practically eating with royalty." He sat straight up in mock arrogance.

Owen didn't want her to leave. He thought about how much fun it was to hang out with Sam over these past few days. It's like the tournament had created some sort of bubble. Everything in his life outside the bubble was crumbling. He couldn't get hold of his wife. His business was falling apart. He had no idea what he was going to do with the rest of his life. But inside the bubble, things were magical. He was having an incredible time hanging out with Sam, excelling at this tournament, and figuring out this secret formula for building successful startups. It had become a little hard to tell which was the real world. He wanted to ask Sam to stay just a bit longer, but he knew that was a bad idea. He just didn't want this to be their last meal together, likely to never see each other again. He didn't want to say good-bye to this magic world. But he reminded himself that continuing to hang out with this beautiful woman could only lead to difficult decisions.

"I swear. Some guy was saying how cool you were at the tables, and there was this tiny brunette chick that kept staring at you the entire time. It's like you have groupies."

"Yeah, one brunette and a bunch of poker onlookers. What a bunch of groupies."

"Hey, come on. The brunette was cute."

"Oh yeah? How cute?"

"Cute enough that I told her to back off. That you prefer blondes."

"Well, actually Sam, I hate to break this to you but I pref—"

"Oh my God! I think I see her at the bar!"

"What?" Owen started to look back to see who Sam was talking about.

"Wait . . . wait . . . don't look!"

Owen turned back to the table before getting a good look at the woman.

"That's only going to encourage her. She's like a stalker or something."

"I've never had one of those." Owen was trying to think about how to take a look at the bar without seeming obvious.

His thoughts were quickly interrupted by Sam's putting her hand on top of his. "You know what I like about you, Owen?"

Uhhh, this was weird. He slowly pulled his hand away. "What?"

Sam leaned in, and started combing Owen's bangs with her fingers. "You are a perfect gentleman who really cares about all this entrepreneurship stuff. Most guys would have tried to make a pass at me or taken advantage of me when I was at my most inebriated. But you are a good guy, Owen."

Owen leaned back in his seat so that her fingers could no longer reach him. Was she trying to make one last move?

"You knew that I was just trying to help you with your business, and I just think your wife is such a lucky woman to have you."

The tournament PA interrupted by announcing that the dinner break would be over in 10 minutes. Players were encouraged to head back to the tables.

"Sam, I'm a little confused."

She smiled and started running her index finger around the rim of her wine glass. She leaned into the table as if she was sharing an important secret. "Women in Vegas are really forward, Owen, and if she thinks we're together, she won't bother making a move. I'm just trying to keep the stalker from thinking she's got a shot."

"Oh. Well, thank you, but I can . . ."

Sam suddenly sat back in her seat and was staring toward the direction of the bar. She spoke through her teeth, trying not to move her lips, "Uh-oh. I think I made her mad."

Owen turned around to see a woman quickly making her way to their table.

Sam, continuing to speak through her teeth, said, "She looks angry."

Owen knew that angry gait all too well. He'd seen it a lot over the past few months. Oh, shit.

And just like that, he felt his magic bubble burst. Owen's real life was now barreling into his oasis. He jumped up from his seat, knowing full well that he had little time to react before Lisa made a scene. "Honey, this isn't what you think! This is my friend, Sam. She's a poker player here, and she thought you were a stranger at the bar . . ."

"SAM?!? This is SAM?!?"

Owen quickly realized what he had just done. He didn't even have an opportunity to take a breath and regroup before Lisa threw her entire glass of Coke in his face.

"Asshole!" She slammed her empty glass on the table, grabbed Sam's bottle of wine by the neck, and stormed off.

Owen grabbed a napkin from the table to wipe off his face and just take a second to regroup. Then, without another word to Sam, he took off after Lisa. He caught up to her in the main hotel pathway, where dozens of people were walking in all different directions.

"Honey!"

Lisa wasn't slowing down, "Don't 'honey' me! I can't believe you did this!"

Owen grabbed Lisa's arm, the one holding the bottle of wine. "Lisa, please. Just give me one minute. Just one minute."

Lisa stopped in the middle of the path, turned to Owen, and crossed her arms. Her eyes were already streaming tears.

"Look. It's not what it looks like. That woman is a friend of mine. Absolutely nothing happened with us. She thought you were a stranger interested in me at the bar and wanted to make you think that I was taken because she thought I was a good guy who was faithful to his wife."

Lisa didn't look like she was buying it . . . but she was still standing there, wiping the tears every few seconds.

"Because I am a good guy, who *is* very faithful to his wife."

They both stood there in silence, just staring at each other. Lisa sniffled. Owen could hear the tournament announcer come back over the speaker to announce that the dinner break was now over and play had resumed. He was sure that Lisa wouldn't understand the implications of the announcement, nor that she would care, even if she knew what it meant.

"Honey, I love you. I promise you. Promise you that I haven't done anything you wouldn't approve of. I have to go back to the tournament. If I make it through today, we are guaranteed at least $300,000."

Lisa didn't reply. She was just standing there, fuming mad. Owen had no idea what to do next. He pulled out his wallet and took out his room key. He put it in her hands and helped her clasp around it. "Look, I'm staying in room 623 upstairs. Here's the key. Please come watch me play or just wait for me in the room. I promise to answer all of your questions as soon as this is over tonight."

Lisa finally looked like she was ready to speak. She stepped a little closer to Owen and spoke to him in a very calm and determined tone, "You told me Sam was a man." She paused. "Not a hot 20-something blonde whose paws were all over you."

Not good. "Lees, I swear to you, nothing happened! She was just giving me business advice, which I can't wait to tell you about. But I have to go back to the tournament. The blinds are so high right now that I can't afford to miss too many hands." He briefly considered assuring Lisa that he thought Sam was well beyond 20-something, but quickly realized that was an atrocious idea.

Lisa was back to mute mode. Owen felt himself incredibly torn. He didn't know what else he could say or do right at this moment, but he *had* to go back to the table. He was already risking his tournament life by not only missing the blinds and antes that he'd be forced to pitch into every hand, but by missing good cards, which were becoming more and more valuable with every hand dealt. This was his only chance to save his company, to get out of debt. He took hold of Lisa's hand again and cupped it with both of his, "I have to go."

He was looking for any kind of approval from her. Anything to make him feel like she'd heard what he said and that he was okay to go back. But she wasn't giving him anything. Just sporadic tears. It was like she knew the stakes and wouldn't give him the slightest indication of what he was looking for.

"I have to go, honey. Please meet me in the room. Room 623."

He got down on his knees in front of her, still holding her hand. "Please be in the room."

Lisa stood there, staring at him, clutching the room key in her hand.

Owen finally got up. "I have to go." He slowly turned around, even though it was the last thing he wanted to do. Every inch of his body was telling him to stay. But his mind was saying "get to the tables, Owen!" He knew that somehow Lisa would soon know the truth—believe the truth—that he wasn't lying about Sam. And, knowing Lisa, that's when the real argument would start, if she found out that he stuck around trying the impossible task of consoling her for hours while simultaneously blowing his chances in the tournament. Rational Lisa—if he ever got to see her again—would agree with this decision. At least that was the assumption Owen had decided to put to the test.

"I love you, baby. So so much." Still no reaction. Feeling like he had no other options, Owen turned and ran back to the tables. It would be two hours until the next 15-minute break.

Chapter 35

Prepare for Bad Luck by Building Up Reserves

O wen was amazed at how lonely he could feel without a cell phone. It was like a fifth limb. It's one thing to be cut off from the world for a couple of hours during a flight, but it's another thing to be cut off for days on end. True, Owen was surrounded by people. And the cameras that were now focusing on every hand would obviously make his face somewhat familiar to poker fans and people who watch ESPN during the day, but the one person he wanted to talk to in the world right then was not in the room.

Lisa had obviously gone through a lot of effort to arrange a last-minute flight and then track down all the details of where he was playing. And for what? He was pretty sure she was still crying somewhere. He just hoped it was in his hotel room. Owen went to check his phone to see how much time before the next break, when he remembered that he couldn't. This was so frustrating. He felt totally helpless.

"Let's go, Biker-Boy."

Owen looked up to see that it was his turn. It wasn't the first time he had zoned out since play resumed, but it was the first time that Masters had said something about it, which meant it was definitely noticeable. Owen looked down at his hand—another mediocre draw of 9-10 off-suit. He was in a pretty late position in the hand, but not late enough to make a call like that, especially now that the table had been rearranged and Masters was right behind him. If play had been difficult before, now it was damn near impossible having to deal with Masters directly to his left. He folded. The dealer shot Owen a look for taking so long and then folding, but who cared about her? She was just worried that this long, boring hand would cut into her screen time.

"Do you have the time?" Owen asked the dealer.

"Quarter after five. You got a bike race to get to or something?" Masters had answered for her and had continued the needling and the nickname Biker-Boy. Fortunately, it had yet to pick up steam around the table, but now it was only a matter of time. Ever since Owen took the big pot before the break, Masters's style had noticeably changed. He wasn't taking as many chances or going into as many pots as before—it definitely seemed as if he was content to cruise-control into the top 27 as the chip leader—and this new laid-back Masters was much more talkative and more lively.

He just started sharing. Owen didn't think he was doing it for the cameras. Masters told the story of how he originally started playing poker, as a way to pay for spare parts for his truck. He left an Ivy League university after one semester because a professor made fun of his habit of dipping tobacco and he hated being the only one that wore cowboy boots to class. One of his favorite things about this tournament had been "the thrill of knocking out people who thought that just because they went to school in Boston, they were God's gift to poker."

Strangely, though, Masters didn't participate in the normal table banter. He'd open up for 30 seconds, a minute tops, and then somebody would ask a follow-up question and he'd give a grunt or one-word response and that was it. End of story time, until some random amount of time later, he'd throw away a hand and start another 30-second soliloquy. These were directed at no one at the table in particular, but they did make Owen feel a little bond with "The Muscle," Masters's WSOP nickname.

Another flop without much action. Another hand over on the turn. Another round of cards—a 2-4 of hearts. Another discard. Another five minutes gone by. Another five minutes closer to the break and going up to the hotel room to see Lisa.

If Lisa was even there.

The next 30 minutes seemed even longer than the first hour and a half. With Masters really letting his foot off the gas, nobody at the table was playing aggressively. This was the world's most elite tournament, and even Owen knew the poker had been subpar. The dealer looked deflated—the dealers changed after the next break, and this table had given her no crazy hands that could possibly put her face on ESPN.

"Dealers. Please finish all current hands and do not deal until . . ."

Finally! Owen didn't wait for the end of announcements. He got up from the table and immediately pulled his phone out to turn it on—true, it was a technical violation, but at the rate he was moving, he'd be 30 feet from the table in the next few seconds.

Of course, the phone had to take forever to turn on . . . and then verify software . . . and then find a cell signal . . . and then unfreeze itself. He'd already pushed the elevator button up when it was finally in full "on" mode. Owen decided to let the elevator pass so he'd keep his signal and see what Lisa had texted him.

He waited for his missed texts to come through. And waited. And waited some more. No texts. No voicemails. This was not promising. Owen couldn't wait any longer. He took the elevator up to the sixth floor, ran to his room, and knocked on the door.

No answer.

He knocked again. He tried the door . . . it was locked. Of course it's locked. It's a hotel room! Deep breaths. Owen slumped against the wall. Now what?

The easy solution was to get another room card from the hotel desk. But that didn't feel right. That felt like defeat. And once he got the card, then what? Just wait for Lisa to show up? And what if she didn't show? How long would he wait?

Then another thought. If he got a new card, that meant invalidating the "lost" one, which meant that if Lisa changed her mind and tried to enter the room after he'd gone back down to the tables, the card he gave her wouldn't work. Shit. Owen took out his phone and dialed her number. It went straight to voicemail.

Owen didn't know how long he'd been slumped against the wall outside the hotel room, but at some point the elevator doors opened. He looked up and saw another guy from the tournament get off, and they exchanged mutual head nods with one another.

Right behind that guy, stepping off the elevator, was Lisa. Owen immediately shot up to embrace her and still had his arms out when she just walked right past him. Not a return hug or even a hello. Lisa stopped in front of the door to the room, opened it up, and then immediately closed it again. And so, there was Owen again. Slumped outside his hotel room; only this time he definitely knew Lisa was inside.

He knocked. He knocked again.

"Lisa. What is it going to take for you to open the door?"

He slapped at the door with his hand.

"Lisa! How long are you going to make me wait out here?"

He knocked a little louder. Nothing. Owen was trying not to get frustrated, but sometimes marriage was so much more difficult than it had to be!

"I know you're mad at me. I know you are so, so mad at me. But I'm telling you the truth—nothing happened. Period! And . . . if I misled you on who or what Sam was, I'm sorry. I'll apologize for that."

A long pause. Owen knocked again. Finally, he heard movement.

"That's it?" She said it through the door without even cracking it open.

"I don't know what else to say, Lisa. There is nothing else to say. Look, okay, in a perfect world, I would never have hung out with Sam. Never even put myself in that position because you weren't around and I knew it would look bad. Yeah, I know you don't think so right now, but I'm a good husband. There are Starbucks I don't go to because the baristas are too flirty and I don't like it. That's corny, I know, but you also know it's the truth." Pause to let that example sink in, "This is not a perfect world. You know that. You showed me ReBicycle's numbers this past week and we both know what they looked like this past month and quarter. I had . . . I had to do something. I felt helpless, like I'm a terrible entrepreneur and terrible husband. And I was freaking out, Lisa. It was driving me nuts."

Another pause. Another regrouping of thoughts.

"Remember that bicycle ride two weeks ago when I came home within 20 minutes and said I had trouble with my back wheel? Remember? Well, that's not entirely the truth. I had a panic attack. I was riding and thinking and breathing hard and then breathing so hard that my head started to spin. I sat down on the side of the road and just stayed there. I didn't . . . I didn't know what to do. And then, I came out here and I— we—have this opportunity and I met Sam, and I found out what she's done and she offered some really good advice. She introduced me to new people. She helped me look at business from a whole new perspective. That's what Sam is all about—we discuss business."

No answer.

"And the God's honest truth is—and I know this sounds crazy, but I'm glad you met her because she's helping us turn ReBicycle around. I wanted you two to meet."

Still no answer. He was tired of talking to a door.

"So that's it."

A check of the phone—he had to get back to the tables. The break was now over. This was getting aggravating.

"Lisa . . . come on. That's it! That's all. Please open the door or at least let me know you're . . . say something at least!!!"

The door swung open. Lisa had changed.

"I'm pregnant."

Boom! She slammed the door closed again.

Chapter 36

Fear and Inaction Are the Two Greatest Threats to Your Business Idea

"S orry."

That was it. A one-word text. This was how Owen and Sam's friendship ended—with a pathetic "sorry." It had been 30 minutes since Lisa had dropped the "news" and Owen still hadn't gone back to the poker tables. He was right outside the doors of the main floor, on a couch. He'd walk around, then almost enter the tournament, but then sit back on the couch. He just couldn't go in. Not yet. Not until he knew something more.

Three times while waiting in the foyer, people had patted him on the shoulder and told him better luck next time—apparently everybody just assumed that a guy hanging right outside the tournament door looking depressed must have just been eliminated. But the real reason was that he needed to talk to Lisa. He kept getting out his cell phone as if it were a magic crystal ball that could somehow deliver the answers, but instead, it had just been silent. Lisa's phone was off—or at least off to him.

Obviously, the whole Lisa situation was serious, but the "news" had brought it to another level. Yes, he had definitely missed several blinds, but that didn't really matter if now there was a child in the picture. His child in the picture. Jesus. What a day. What a week.

And during this wait, Sam had texted him. He hadn't thought much about Sam in the past couple of hours. Who would have? And now, in Owen's mind, she was associated with ReBicycle, and that was business and definitely not what he was focused on now. Still, she was somebody he knew, someone he felt that he could trust. After a couple more fruitless moments of waiting for something— anything—Owen texted Sam back.

"Need help. She's still angry."

"How angry?"

"She's pregnant."

It wasn't three seconds after sending the text that Owen's phone rang.

"Are you serious?"

"Serious as a heart attack."

"Well, congratulations to you two."

"Don't congratulate me yet, Sam. She's still pissed and won't talk to me."

"From this afternoon or from something else?"

"This afternoon." For such a smart person, that was certainly a dumb question. "I've explained to her who you are and that nothing happened between us, but I don't know. Maybe it's the pregnancy, maybe it's Vegas, but right now she isn't having anything to do with me."

"So what are you going to do, Owen?"

"Well, for the time being, I've been standing in the lobby, calling Lisa and waiting for a response . . . any suggestions?"

"Give her some time."

"I don't have time, Sam! I can't play poker right now in this mind-set! I need to do something."

"Well, then, do something."

"What?"

There was an exasperated sigh on the other end.

"Men."

"Oh, come on, Sam. Give me some advice."

"My advice is to get back to the poker table."

"That's it?"

"Listen, Owen. I'm at the airport. My flight leaves in 30 minutes. Call me or e-mail me if you have any questions about ReBicycle. I think you've got something. I didn't when we first met. But now . . . you might."

"Yeah, thanks."

"Hey, by the way, where is Lisa now?"

"She's taken over my hotel room."

"And you tried to get her to let you in?"

"She won't let me. I tried getting another copy of a room key made and she had the deadbolt on the door. She's intent on not letting me in."

"Get to the poker tables, Owen."

"Have a good flight, Sam."

A long pause.

"Sorry, Owen. Just don't be frozen with fear. Do something, even if it turns out not to have been the right thing."

Chapter 37

Understand Your Tendencies On Tilt So That You Can Compensate for Them

S am was right, dammit! Get back to the tables. Play like a man possessed for the next hour or whatever! Leave with the chip lead tonight and be able to knock on that door and say to Lisa that you're going to the second-to-final table!

But first, one more look at the cell phone. Nothing. Fine. Power off. Back into the black. Owen returned to the floor and couldn't believe how much it had shrunk. One, two, three, four. That was it. Four tables left. That's only 36 players left, max, and he could see that one of the tables already had two empty seats and another table had one empty seat—33 people left.

It could have been down to 32 if Owen had stayed away another hour. At first, he thought that his seat had been moved after the break because the chip pile in front of his old seat didn't resemble the one he had left. But no, that was it. Did somebody steal some chips? Of course, they wouldn't. There were far too many cameras for that. It had to be accurate. Damn, these blinds were brutal.

At the top of Owen's chip pile—though *pile* was now a generous word—there were several $50,000 chips. That was good. But every other chip underneath those big chips was tiny. Like inconsequentially tiny. It was pointless to count them, he'd have to go all-in soon, and judging by the quick glances from the other players, they all knew it.

There were a couple of new players at the table. Their faces looked familiar, but by this point the line had blurred between players Owen had seen before on TV and players he had seen earlier in the tournament. One of the guys was wearing a polo from a poker web site and spoke with a British accent. He was almost certainly a pro. The other guy Owen was not too sure about. He looked about as confident as Owen felt on the inside but still had a pretty good chip pile in front of him. Must be doing something right. And where was Masters? Yes! Finally moved to a different table. That was the good news.

The bad news was that Owen was definitely on tilt now. Players on tilt are those who either get too emotionally lost in the game or are too low on chips to continue playing with the same level of strategy as before. A lot of times, it's both—a player is angry and stunned that he just lost 90 percent of his chips on a bad beat, so he decides that he doesn't have a real shot and goes all-in on a mediocre hand. Players on tilt are relying a lot more on luck than skill to carry them through the day. And as it happens virtually every time, their luck eventually runs out.

That's the classic definition of "on tilt," but Owen played on tilt differently. He became more conservative, more doubtful of his reads. His likely fate was to just be blinded out of the tournament, meaning that he would be too hesitant to act until the blinds had gone around enough times that he'd eventually be out of chips. It was important to know these things about yourself. How you react to situations that seem hopeless.

Owen hadn't even realized that he was operating on tilt with ReBicycle these past few months. But now that he was thinking about the pattern, he could disrupt his natural tendencies. There were only three hands before he'd be in the small blind, meaning if he didn't make a move in the next five hands, he'd fall under $150,000 or so in chips, and that would likely mean the end of the tournament. He still had enough time and chips to recover. Barely.

Owen braced himself for his next hand. Breathe, Owen.

Like using a porta-potty, he knew the cards he'd have to play might not be pretty, but he might have to play them out of necessity. He peeked at the cards one at a time. The first one was a queen. Good start. He'd take a face card. And the second card was . . . also a queen. Pocket queens! Wow, great start. He looked around the table again. Action was light—people were waiting to see what he'd do. The mousy guy made a mousy raise (figures) and two other players called.

So not only did he have a good hand, but he had some action. It didn't take him long to act. He took half of his chip pile and shoved it toward the dealer.

"Raise."

A couple of seconds later, the dealer finished counting. It was $190,000 in chips. More than Owen had thought; maybe counting the chips wouldn't have been such a bad idea. It was a raise of $100,000. Two quick folds and then a long look from the player in the big blind. Owen was trying his best to look like a guy who was bluffing but trying not to look like he was bluffing. It was like a triple-bluff, and after a second he chuckled to himself. Whatever. The

guy would call or fold, regardless of how he blinked. Owen decided
to count his remaining chips.

"Raise."

"How much?" The dealer looked at the guy in the big blind. He
had a jet-black goatee. Like every other player, he looked familiar,
but then again, maybe Owen had just seen him on a box of Just for
Men. He nodded at Owen while talking to the dealer.

"How much does he have left?"

"A chip count, sir."

Owen finished counting the small chips. There were more than
he thought.

"I've got 200 grand here."

"I raise $200,000."

Mr. Goatee was forcing the all-in. Damn, Owen realized he
must have been marked as all-but-dead. And now the big problem
was if Mr. Goatee had a king or an ace and hit it on the flop,
that was it. Tournament over within his first hand after the break.

Owen knew that his natural tendency would be to fold. He
was scared of getting knocked out, and he hated being in a position
where someone already thought they had him beat. But if he had
learned anything in the past few days from his customer interviews,
it was that even if you think there's no shot, that you are doomed to
fail, but you still have time left to play, you need to give it a try. You
can't win unless you play this hand, Owen. Take the shot.

"All-in." Owen pushed the rest of his chips toward the middle.
He kept his queens face down, though—since there might be other
players in the hand who would continue to play one another for a
side pot.

"Call."

"Call."

Two more calls. This was going to be a four-way all-in pot. Well,
the only player that was actually all-in was Owen. All the other callers
had decent chip piles, so even if they lost, they wouldn't be out of
the tournament.

The flop came: king of hearts, 10 of hearts, 2 of clubs.

Owen's breath stopped. He couldn't take his eyes off the king. He tried not to stare at it but couldn't help it—this was it. That old man with the crown on his head was like his executioner. He knew. He absolutely knew it.

But strangely, Owen was at peace. He was comfortable with losing this hand because he knew he had played it right. As long as you focus on making the right moves, you will do well. You might lose every now and then when the flop has an unlucky king, but the majority of the time you're going to come out ahead. Owen thought about how he had played this hand better than the one against Masters. Strangely, he'd feel better about losing this hand than getting lucky against Masters after he had misread the situation.

The turn was a 4 of clubs and the river was a 7 of spades. A pretty dry flop besides the king, and the side-betting pile was small.

"Gentlemen, please show your cards."

Big blind went first. 9-10 of hearts. Owen had beat him . . . barely. The other caller had an ace-2. A loser to the queens this time. Owen's eyes immediately focused on Mousy. He was staring at Owen as if daring him to turn his cards over first. Owen did. There were a couple of gasps from the crowd at the queens—it made Owen realize there was a crowd again. Instantly, he got a little tense thinking of that. But all eyes were on Mousy. He peeked at his cards one more time and flipped them.

Ace-queen.

Owen's queens had taken it—and the $1.2 million pot. He took a deep breath. All right—he was pretty much guaranteed to see this hand on television in a couple of months. Owen was about to smile when . . .

"Whoa!" There was an explosion of noise one table over. Greg Masters's table. And before Owen even realized what was going on, he saw Annie Duke stand up. She had been the second-to-last female in the tournament. Not anymore; 32 players left. Five more to go for the night.

That's too bad, Owen thought. He liked Annie. Lisa liked Annie. Annie Duke was probably the only player Lisa could actually name.

And suddenly Lisa came flooding back. Damn! A $1.2 million pot and it didn't mean a damn thing to Lisa because she hadn't been here to see it. He was still in big trouble.

Why can't he seem to catch a break like this in his personal life? He thought about how pissed Lisa was. Pregnant Lisa. Deep breath. $1.2 million pot. New hand. Focus on the positives. See how you can shorten this night and still have time to make things up with Lisa. More than winning the hand, Owen knew that revealing the queens made him look conservative and lucky. He could exploit that now that there were new players at the table and they didn't know his style. Quick look around the table. No easy outs here. Every player had moved on from the hand.

Except Mousy. He looked like he was about to vomit. He was demonstrating all the signs of a player on tilt.

Target acquired.

Chapter 38

There Is No Mistaking It When You Uncover Migraine Problems Worth Solving

K nock. Knock.

Darkness. Complete and utter darkness. What the hell was going on? Owen stumbled for his phone. 6:05. . . ohhhhhhh, he still felt groggy. Maybe one snooze of the alarm.

Knock. Knock.

Okay, there was definitely somebody at the door . . . Lisa! Owen snapped out of bed and ran to open the door.

The gentleman at the door looked startled at the force with which Owen flung it open. He definitely wasn't Lisa.

"Umm . . . Mr. Chase? Your 6:00 A.M. wake-up with breakfast and paper."

"Oh . . . I didn't order breakfast."

"Complimentary for this room, Mr. Chase. May I?"

Owen realized he was blocking the door—and that all he had on was his boxers. There was also a throbbing pain coming again from his leg. He had definitely jolted up too quickly.

"Yes. Come in . . . just set it there." Owen hobbled around his bed to find his pants for a dollar or two. He realized he should probably just put his pants on while he had them in hand, "Uh. You don't happen to have any aspirin do you? For my leg."

"Mr. Chase, there is a basic first-aid kit in the medicine cabinet. Would you like me to get it for you?"

"That's all right. Thank you."

"Mr. Chase, several reporters have inquired whether you'd be interested in doing interviews before today's play starts."

"Reporters?"

"ESPN. *Wall Street Journal*. Couple of others."

"Uh . . . no . . . actually. Just . . . maybe later. Not this morning."

"A couple of them left cards. I'll just leave them on the tray for you."

"Thanks."

"And Mr. Chase, good luck today. I'm rooting for you."

"Ha. Thanks, man." Owen handed him a five. He could get used to this new celebrity treatment. Something had definitely changed since he had made it to the top 27. Now, a lot of people knew him. On the way back to the room last night, he must have been approached, what, five or six times? More than a couple. They all knew his name. And the hotel had comped him this suite. And now the breakfast.

All this special treatment was nice, but it didn't seem to make up for the fact that he was still alone in this room and his pregnant wife was somewhere else, upset or angry or contemplating divorce. Actually, she was still probably asleep. He had slipped a note under her door last night in a last attempt to apologize. There was nothing more he could do. He resolved to let her make the next move.

Plus, Owen had work to do. As hard as it was to stop thinking about Lisa, this could be his last opportunity to find out if there was any hope for ReBicycle.

He went over to the huge, sturdy desk. Everything in the suite was gigantic. He looked for the sheet on which he'd written down some leads last night. The sun was just rising over the strip, and from his high floor, Owen could see the tips of the Sierra Madres in the distance. It was that rarest of rare moments in Vegas—a scene that is naturally beautiful. Logically, he knew it was a beautiful scene, but emotionally he couldn't digest one. Just too much uncertainty floating around his head. Uncertain marriage. Uncertain business. Uncertain cards. Uncertain life.

Owen poured himself a cup of coffee. The list had 15 names of bike share programs Stephanie wasn't able to reach the day before. Owen had purposefully asked her not to reveal how the calls she was able to connect went. He didn't want it to prejudice his own interviews.

The first call was to the college town of Syracuse, New York, which had not only been one of the first cities to pop up when Owen had googled "bike share programs," but was one of the only cities that seemed to have a paid, dedicated staffer running the program.

". . . I don't know how accurate that is now, but yeah, when we first started, and I was given this job, there was like nobody to talk to about these kinds of programs. I ended up talking to a lot of Brits and Irish city planners, and that's who we modeled our program after."

Owen had Jim Reesing on the line. Reesing was the Syracuse, New York, Director of Non-Motorized Transportation. While he was initially wary of talking to Owen, Owen was able to really get him to open up by dropping Shawn Malloy's name and explaining that he wasn't selling anything. These interviews were becoming second nature to Owen. He was actually having fun.

And over the next two hours, Owen found that a lot of these city planners had worked long, long hours and got very little credit for starting their bike share program from scratch, and they were excited to have someone asking them questions about their work. Dammit, did they want to talk about it!

There was an amazing difference in conversations between bike store customers who didn't identify with a problem and bike share executives who truly had a migraine problem. Owen found himself acting more like a psychiatrist, just talking to guys like Reesing and another fellow he recommended from Savannah, and then another two guys that guy said to talk to from Tampa and Gainesville, Florida. Without any prompting, they all spoke at length about the problem of sourcing those damn bikes. Also, they all spoke quite reverently about Shawn Malloy. Apparently, Owen had been talking to the guy who set the standard across the country without even realizing it.

Owen took his time and made sure he got all of the important questions answered. He confirmed that both for-profit and non-profit bike share programs experienced the same issues in sourcing bikes. He made sure that they had each tried other solutions to this problem. And he confirmed that they had dedicated budgets they could spend if presented with the right alternative. Fifteen hundred dollars seemed to be a magic number for them.

At 9:30 A.M. Owen looked down. The extra-sturdy desk was covered in observations he'd written down, scraps of quotes and follow-up questions he'd written on the fly. The breakfast was still untouched. He picked up one scrap of paper. He'd written down, "Q: Did Reesing ever speak to his overseas manufacturer about the quality? A: Manufacturer said would need new designs . . . Reesing did not follow up since he's not designer." Right below it, Owen had listed another question, "Q: Has Reesing been approached by anyone else offering a solution? A: Yes! One Euro supplier wanted to start from scratch w/ new stations, payments, etc. Offer was 8x budget!!" Above several of the pieces of paper Owen had written the same word in all caps—"PIECEMEAL!"

That was essentially what every bike share program he'd talked to that morning had to do. They all had to piecemeal the equipment they needed from different companies. There was no standard across the board. From Syracuse to Tampa, San Antonio to Eugene, every city had to get bikes in one place, or two or three places, replacement parts from another place, repairs done by a third party.

And the worst part was that some of the programs that were relying on three or four separate vendors ended up spending a ridiculous amount per bike. Like way more than Owen felt comfortable about as a taxpayer. It was ridiculous!

It was addictive talking to these guys. They totally loved that Owen understood their problem, and Owen totally loved their answers. So this is what happens when you actually find a migraine?!

Another look at his phone. Time for one more phone call.

Chapter 39

Get Comfortable with Being Wrong

"Owen!"

Flash. Snap.

"Mr. Chase! Over here!"

More flashes and snaps from the other direction.

"Mr. Chase, do you have a lawyer?"

Suddenly, Owen felt a firm hand grab his left elbow and instinctively pulled it away. But the hand stayed put and a large man in a nice suit, earpiece, and greased hair said firmly, "This way, Mr. Chase."

Apparently, now the hotel had given him security. Unbelievable. He wasn't even to the final table yet. Owen kept waiting for his heart to start beating—to feel nervous. After all, he should feel nervous! But he didn't. Honestly, he wanted to go make some more phone calls about ReBicycle. He was tired of poker. There had been so damn much of it! Okay, not that tired of poker, but it was tough to try and refocus on poker after this morning and with things still up in the air with Lisa.

Unlike a lot of people, both at the tables and in the audience today, he understood that today wasn't the be-all and end-all of his life. It was a chance for 27 people who had already earned a ridiculous amount of money to earn a more ridiculous amount. That's what it was. Over 7,000 people down to 27. It was a rat race that took equal parts strategic play, gutsy moves, good luck, and good timing.

Apparently, now it was all about branding and self-promotion. Like, a lot of it. When Owen walked out of his hotel room in the morning, he stumbled over no less than five gift bags placed in front of his door. They were all different, but essentially contained the same ingredients—a really nice bottle of liquor or cologne, a piece of jewelry, a load of gift certificates, and an engraved card telling him to enjoy the gifts. And, oh, by the way, would he consider wearing the branded shirt that was also in the bag to the tournament today? Pretty please.

But no. He'd already picked out his shirt for today. It was the same one he had worn the day after the bike accident. More than any other day, it was that day that had turned things around for him. It just felt right. It was also the day he started digging himself out of the hole that was ReBicycle 1.0. That's how he now labeled the pre-Vegas business model for ReBicycle. Wearing that shirt wasn't about luck; it was a commitment to the future, a celebration of what's to come. Plus, he didn't really like the jewelry or cologne.

The security detail cleared a path in front of Owen, but it was more for show than anything. He didn't actually keep anyone from approaching Owen. One guy held out a WSOP hat as Owen was walking by, and Owen took it and thanked him. Owen had already made it several steps forward when he heard the guy yell, "You gonna sign it or just steal it?" Owen hadn't realized the guy was looking for an autograph. That was a shocker. He got a silver sharpie from the security guy (at least he was prepared for the important stuff) and signed the hat, "Sorry I almost stole your hat! – O." That was just weird.

When Owen entered the tournament floor, he scanned the room for Lisa. Nothing. He kept scanning, waiting to hear her familiar voice. For some reason he imagined the scene from *Rocky* where Adrian sneaks through the ropes into the ring past security. He kept waiting for her to emerge out of the crowd and replay that scene, but she wasn't there.

Out of the 27 people left in the tournament, there was a handful Owen already recognized. Greg Masters was there with a pile of chips that looked like it had cloned itself into another equally large pile of chips. There was no mistaking Chris "Jesus" Ferguson, a pro player who had long hair, a beard (hence the nickname Jesus), and a bracelet signifying that he'd already won this thing more than a decade ago. On television, he always appeared in the hunt, and this year was no different, though his stack wasn't that much bigger than Owen's. The second-smallest stack at right around $1 million belonged to the only female left—Vanessa Selbst. By far the smallest stack was that of John Pho, the son of a Vietnamese businessman. He had worn the same Columbia University T-shirt the entire tournament. It looked disgusting, but Owen still liked it better than the hoodie style all the other kids were wearing.

Ever since the young Dane, Peter Eastgate, had won the WSOP at age 22, it had become de rigueur for every player under 25 to wear a hoodie and ear-buds. It was like competing against a zombie. They never contributed to the table discussion, never showed their cards unless they absolutely had to, and never acted like humans. They were robots, and judging by the number of hoodies around the three tables, there were about six robots left.

And then there was Phil Helmuth. Owen heard him before he saw him and, sure enough, he was wearing the bracelet he'd earned at this tournament in 1989. From television, Owen knew that sometimes Phil was really quiet and other times he was a live one. Today, he looked to be a live one. The chair next to Phil was empty, and Owen felt bad for the poor sap that had to sit next to him. It would be at least a few more minutes until one of the tournament officials let Owen know that he was the poor sap.

So that's how this day would begin—seated next to a guy with a World Series of Poker bracelet and a personality that reminded Owen about it every 10 seconds. Owen now really wanted to be back in the hotel room, making phone calls.

Play was to begin at 11 A.M., but due to technical difficulties with the cameras, they pushed back the start time 20 minutes. Some of the players bolted, while others seemed content to sit at the table in deep concentration. Owen didn't know what he should do. Get some coffee?

"Mr. Chase, can we have a moment?" It was the ESPN producer from three days ago who had decided Owen wasn't worth an interview. Apparently, he was interesting enough now.

"Certainly."

"Thanks. Give my cameraman a minute. I'm going to ask you about the tournament today, how you feel, how you got here. A little about you. Won't be long. We good, Mike?" He looked at the camera guy, got a nod, and mouthed three-two and . . .

"Welcome back to Round 7 of the World Series of Poker. I'm here with what, well, I can only describe as one of the most unlikely survivors in a year of unlikely survivors—Owen Chase. Owen, how would you describe your path here?"

"Luck."

"Ha!" Nice big fake laugh, "That's great. What else. What's been your key to success?"

"Honestly, not focusing on poker the whole time. I think having other distractions helped me from getting too emotionally invested in the individual hands. I was able to be more objective and make the right strategic moves."

"And is that your key today?"

"Yeah. Sure. That's the thing, though. There is no key. I mean, I should have been eliminated several times by now, but I got cards when I needed them, and meanwhile, there are people like Annie Duke or Phil Ivey who spent years perfecting poker and probably played every hand exactly right and still lost."

"That's so true." Nice big fake compassion. "So your goal is not perfect play?"

"I've just become very comfortable over the week or so with being wrong. That comfort level keeps me from going on tilt or operating out of fear. I mean, just because those pros are no longer in the tournament doesn't mean they aren't incredible poker players. So I just try to follow their lead and minimize my losses when I'm wrong so that I can live to play another hand."

"That sounds good, Owen. And what do you do for a living?"

"I own a bike store. We take gently used or leftover bike parts and craft unique, high-quality bicycles. The web site is www. rebic—"

The interviewer cut him off before he could finish the address, "And what happens if you win this thing?"

"I'll continue to work with bicycles. I love them."

"And if you don't win?"

"I'll have no regrets. Look, I've got no false dreams about competing against guys like Masters. My plan is to wait until I have a great hand and put it all on the line. If I do that, whatever happens, I'll be happy."

"Biking must have made you philosophical."

"No. Just poor."

"Ha!" The interviewer gave Owen a genuine laugh and quickly regained his composure. All within the span of maybe half a second.

"One last question, Mr. Chase. Are you going to try to get your kid involved in poker at an early age?"

"My kid?"

"Yeah, we talked to your wife earlier. She said you two were expec . . . wawawawawawawaa."

Owen immediately zoned out the interviewer. Lisa was here! Somewhere on the floor. Where was she?

"Lisa!"

No answer. He turned around scanning the crowd.

"LISA!" He saw her a few feet away and ran up to her.

She was standing in front of an Auntie Anne's Pretzel stand, not exactly the set Owen had imagined for their reunion. "You're here."

"Well, where did you think I would be? I'm pregnant. Eating for two now, and all that."

"I don't even know what to say right now. You. Me. Vegas. Pregnant."

"This pretzel is pretty good. Do you want some?"

"Yeah, thanks." Owen grabbed a big bite, "So you're into pretzels now, huh?"

"Shouldn't you be playing poker right now?"

"Like in 10 minutes."

"Yeah? You doing good?"

"Of course, I'm doing good. Well, you know, I'm doing okay. I'm hanging in there."

"That's what the ESPN guy said."

"Yeah? How did he find you?"

"I found him. I asked him if he'd seen you and he said no. Then he asked me who I was and I told him."

"What else did you tell him?"

"That I'm naming the child goldenpalace.com. I heard there might be some sort of incentives to do that here."

"What did you really tell him?"

He grabbed another bite of pretzel. It was stupid to miss breakfast.

"I don't know. Nothing big. That we were expecting our first kid. Things like that. Sooo . . . I talked to Sam."

Owen managed not to spit the pretzel out. "Yeah?"

"She cleared up a lot of things for me . . . she's really smart about business, you know."

"Yeah, I know."

"Hey," she said with the enthusiasm of someone who was about to say something really important. "Do you want to split another pretzel? I'm still hungry."

"You read my mind." He could almost hear the ice breaking.

Of course, Owen had a ton of questions to ask Lisa about how, why, and when she talked to Sam. He was bursting to know. But now was definitely not the time. Lisa was in a good mood and she was here talking to him. That was enough. Plus, Owen had poker to play. A lot of it today. They started walking toward the tables, eating the second pretzel, which somehow tasted much worse than the first. But it didn't matter. Lisa was content. Or acting content.

"You wanna know what we talked about, don't you?"

"Noooo." Owen shook his head.

"You're a terrible liar!"

"Yeah? You have terrible taste in pretzels." Pause, "It must have been good, whatever it was, for you not to be mad anymore."

"Who said I'm not mad anymore? I got some sleep last night. I'm well rested. I'm away from the school and enjoying Vegas, but that doesn't mean I'm not mad. I'm just more confident about Sam. You, on the other hand . . . the jury is still out." She gave him a little smile.

"Man, you know how to give a guy a pep talk."

"How's this? The note was good. Keep it up. It's a good start."

A tap on the shoulder. The floor boss, "Mr. Chase, two minutes to start. You need to take your seat."

"Good luck, O."

Chapter 40

Don't Go All-In without Confirming Your Assumptions through Smaller Bets

It was getting late, but Owen still felt the adrenaline coursing through his body. Only 16 players left. The crowd was huge now. The field of hundreds of tables from that first day, which seemed like months ago now, had been whittled down to just two and, thankfully, Masters was at the other table. On the other hand, Owen still had Phil Helmuth to deal with. Seven hours after Owen bluffed him out of a lot of chips, Phil was still sour about misreading it.

The dinner break was . . . well, perfect, in a word. Dinner with Sam had been nice. She was new and interesting, and there was a lot to learn, but dinner with Lisa was so much better. Sure, they talked about business, but they also talked about life and their plans for the future. It was just so much more fulfilling. Owen hadn't even realized how a week of poker and interviews had warped his mind. This was the reality check he needed. The fact that there was also a physical check of at least $750,000 waiting for him didn't hurt.

The baby was due around February 15. That would certainly make Valentine's Day interesting this year. Owen showed Lisa his bum knee and the pictures he'd taken on his camera phone right after the accident. He explained to her what happened and how he realized that the business was failing. He told her how Sam had helped him figure out that customers didn't actually want ReBicycle and how they'd met Shawn Malloy and all the calls Owen had made to the different bike shares. Lisa had a ton of questions, but they were the good kind. She was interested. Skeptical but interested. She was most interested in the part where they would try to sell the new product before investing any more money.

They talked about poker. Owen had to explain that the final table of the tournament wouldn't be played until four months from now. ESPN liked to tease months of WSOP footage to get people excited about the final table, which would be played live. So no matter what, today would be his last day of poker for some time.

It wasn't until dessert that Lisa finally shared about her conversation with Sam. Apparently, Sam had felt bad about witnessing—and perhaps even instigating—that blow up and knew that Lisa was staying at the hotel. She called Lisa from the airport, apologized for what had happened, and then they "talked." When Owen pressed Lisa further, though, nothing. All Lisa would say is "we talked, and I feel better."

"And so then you don't have an issue with my calling Sam and bouncing ideas off of her?"

"I'm not saying you two should become best friends, but do I see the value she brings to our business."

That was a very politically correct way of saying feel free to call her, but no funny business! Owen got the hint and made a mental note to call Sam tomorrow. He was still making notes at the poker table of questions he'd forgotten to ask her. He'd left that piece of paper at the table. He didn't want to go back. But now it was almost over. Sixteen players. Two tables. Roughly $1.5 million in chips and one pouty Phil Helmuth.

And Phil hadn't been having the best go of it. He was hurting, and if there's one thing worse than a pouty poker player, it's one who's also complaining about his terrible luck. Still, Helmuth somehow seemed to find the chips to call Owen every time he made a move. Helmuth was way too big a pro to play on tilt. Right?

It was 10:30 P.M. The next break was still 30 minutes away when Owen checked his hand and saw a pocket pair of 8s. It was a good starting hand, but one that could quickly turn mediocre if there were too many players in the hand. Owen bet $100,000. He thought about how funny it was that just a few days ago he started the tournament with just $30,000 in chips, and now a 100K bet was just a small portion of his stack.

"Let me guess, 5–7 again?" Helmuth was complaining.

"Hey, you know, it's a lucky hand for me, why not play it?"

"It's about time you gave me those chips back. I call."

Owen could feel a tension in the air, or maybe everyone was just ready for the night to end. Either way, all of the other players at the table got out of the hand. If this was an old Western, a whistle would be heard and a tumbleweed would have rolled between them because it was finally time to have the shootout at the saloon.

Flop: 8 of hearts, jack of diamonds, jack of spades. Owen looked coolly at Phil. With a full house, the key was to try and get as many of his chips in the pot as possible, but to do so in the most casual way possible. Owen tapped the table to signal that he was checking. Phil checked as well. That hadn't been the move Owen was anticipating. Maybe this wouldn't be the shootout after all.

The turn card was a 6 of hearts. Not a strong enough card to bet by itself. That put Owen in the position again of having to check; otherwise, he might give away his position. No sooner had Owen's hand touched the felt than he heard Phil shout, "all-in!"

Phil just sat there, allowing his announcement to soak in. When he felt satisfied that it had made enough of a splash, Phil finally pushed his chips toward the center of the table. Owen glanced at him. He'd been waiting for this moment all day.

In his best Phil Helmuth impression, Owen commanded, "Well, count it, and tell me how much it is." He heard a roar of surprised laughter behind him. That turned into a brief but excited round of applause punctuated by a "Get 'em, Biker-Boy!" from somewhere deep in the crowd.

Phil had no other option but to comply. That was enjoyable, watching Phil sourly count his remaining chips.

"$430,000."

"I call."

Phil flipped his cards—pocket 6s.

"6s full of jacks." The crowd oohed.

Owen let the ooohs sink in. He wanted to look like he'd gotten beat. Let Phil really enjoy the moment for a minute.

"Well, Tricycle-Boy," Phil taunted, "you had to take off the training wheels eventually."

And that line! That exact moment! That's what Owen was waiting for. In the week of playing in the tournament, Owen had heard the sporadic crowd make a lot of different cheering sounds. But when he flipped over his pocket 8s, it was the first time he'd heard the crowd totally lose it. A wall of noise filled the hall.

"Eights full of jacks. Owen Chase eliminates—" The crowd drowned out the rest. Phil Helmuth, the last remaining bracelet winner still in the tournament was eliminated. Fifteen players left. Six to go.

Chapter 41

Second Chances Are Rare—Make Sure You Get It Right the First Time Around

There was a tinge of guilt in drinking champagne and knowing that Lisa couldn't have any. But she was asleep and Owen had earned his right to celebrate.

Play had lasted only 90 minutes after the 11 P.M. break. Greg Masters had gone on a tear and single-handedly eliminated three people from the other table. Nicholas the Parisian was the 10th to go, and right after midnight, it became official—Owen Chase had made it to the final table of the World Series of Poker. The final table!

The hotel or the tournament or whomever had been nice enough to send up this bottle of champagne to his room, and it would be a waste to just leave it in the suite. With Lisa sleeping 10 feet away and his next hand of poker still four months away, life felt good. Complete wasn't quite right because he had a long way to go. Reset was more like it. Owen was feeling reset and it felt right.

Owen got out his phone and saw several congratulatory texts. News had spread fast. Pitchford had even sent him "8=====>" which was their inside way of saying "great freaking job!" followed by "Easiest money I've ever won in poker :)." Owen was more than happy to split the guaranteed $1.1 million. He had gotten so much more out of this week than the cash, and none of it would have happened if not for Pitchford.

It seemed like so much money, and yet, after the taxes, Owen's half would still not be able to cover all of his losses from ReBicycle. That was an incredible thought. How could he have spent so much money going so far in the wrong direction? Oh well. He finished his glass of champagne and quickly refilled it. That was a different Owen, and he'd never make that same mistake again. It had taken ReBicycle a year to burn through over $600K and yet, in one week, Owen had almost earned it all back.

Owen knew that he didn't just win a seat at the final table— he'd won himself a second chance. No one gets that kind of opportunity. A reboot of a startup. Of trying to build something that makes the world a little bit better. That solves a serious need out there. He wasn't going to squander this second chance.

Owen felt the phone buzzing in his pocket. Another text. This time from Sam.

"Congrats."

"Thanks . . . I couldn't have done it without you!"

Owen took a swig of the champagne directly from the bottle. Another buzz. Sam's response.

"I know."

Chapter 42

Even When You Find a Migraine Problem, Crafting a Solution Requires Vigilance and Readjustment

Four months. Had it really been four months? It felt like Owen was just here last week. Same billboards, same signs offering the same "amazing deals." The only thing that was noticeably different was the November climate. It was cool and refreshing.

"Man, I never tire of this city. It's the only place in the States where you can—"

Lisa whipped around from the passenger seat of the cab and locked in on Pitchford. "Where you can what?" She gave him a big grin, like she wasn't letting him off the hook until he completed the sentence.

Pitchford stared back at Lisa, searching through his mental Rolodex of possible alternatives to what he actually meant to say, but it was clear that he was having trouble coming up with anything good. "Where you can . . . it's just got the best food."

Lisa shook her head and gave him a big smile. "Weak." She didn't seem to enjoy Pitchford's sense of humor the way Owen did, but she found him endearing all the same.

"Seriously, more five-star restaurants per capita than any city."

Stepping into the Rio felt like walking into a high school reunion. Now that Owen was one of the nine finalists, there was already a large swarm of people to greet him as he exited the taxi.

"Mr. Chase, please accept this gift from . . ."

"Mr. Chase, I'd like to offer you and your wife the pleasure of dining at the . . ."

"Mr. Chase. You golf, right? How about a . . ."

There must have been 20 coupons and gift cards pressed into his hands. A mob was starting to form around him and Lisa. He couldn't tell if she liked it or not, but it had to impress her. As they walked toward the check-in desk, a hotel concierge ran up to stop them. "Mr. Chase, you don't need to do that. Your hotel suite is already ready. We'll have you sign something in your room to check in. This way, please." Yeah . . . Lisa had to definitely be impressed now. And Pitchford, well . . . where did he go? He'd already disappeared.

After settling in the room and taking a quick nap, it was time for dinner. Owen let Lisa choose the spot. After reading a lot of online reviews and flipping through the guidebooks in their suite, she finally chose Il Greco.

"Why does that restaurant sound familiar?"

"It's just a few blocks from the Rio. Italian. Known for their desserts."

And then it hit Owen. Il Greco was the restaurant where he and Sam had dinner after she'd been knocked out of the tournament. Yeah, he was sure of it. The dessert. The food. The location. That was the night that Sam tried to kiss him.

"Owen. Honey. You okay? Are you good with Il Greco?"

"Uh . . . sure."

"Give me five minutes to get ready."

Owen lay back on the bed. So much had changed since Il Greco.

And it all came back to him as soon as he entered the Il Greco foyer. Owen had not spoken to Sam since Vegas. She'd swooped into his life, rearranged the way he was thinking and doing business, and then within one week, boom, she was gone. It was like an act of nature—Hurricane Sam.

Tonight was going to be very different, though. He was at a much different place with his poker game, with his business, and most importantly, with his marriage. Owen was looking forward to showing off for Lisa over the next few days. Tonight would be no exception.

As soon as he and Lisa were shown to their table, Owen started making recommendations from the menu. "The Madeira is pretty good here. But I think you'll really enjoy the desserts."

Lisa seemed grateful for the suggestion but was still carefully inspecting the oversized menu. Owen was happy to give her all the time she needed.

He thought he heard someone say his name from across the room and looked behind his shoulder for someone carrying a camera. Perhaps it was one of the many fans here this week. Maybe they'd want an autograph.

"Owen!"

Owen looked over his other shoulder, still having trouble identifying the direction from which he was being summoned. And there she was.

"Sam?!"

"Yep. Still my name."

"Sam!"

"Hey."

"How the . . . what the . . .?"

He got up from the table and they shared an awkward hug and then a moment of silence as they checked each other out. Not in a sexual way, but in that way that you do after you haven't seen some-body for a while, making sure that they have all of their appendages and no weird tattoos or whatever. The human nature check. Finally, it was Lisa who broke the ice.

"Hey, Sam! What a small world!" Sam ran over to Lisa's side of the table and gave her a big hug.

"No kidding!"

"How are you, Sam?" Lisa asked. "You look fabulous."

"Still doing a lot of running?" Owen asked. He wasn't sure if that was an okay thing for him to ask in front of Lisa, but she didn't give him any looks, so it was probably fine. He made a mental note not to say anything else flattering about Sam's appearance to his six-months-pregnant-and-just-beginning-to-show wife.

"Actually, running less. I gave up alcohol after the tournament and, get this, started cycling."

"That's fantastic!" Lisa exclaimed.

"So what are you doing in Vegas, Sam? Why didn't you let me know you'd be here?"

"Well, I didn't want to distract you and . . . well . . ."

"Hey, is that Biker-Boy?" Greg Masters came up behind Sam and shook Owen's hand. It was like a four-month reunion. Owen had never really talked to Greg besides a few head nods, but now he felt obliged to say something. Anything.

"You ready for tomorrow, Greg? Hell of a break."

"Yeah, I'm ready to get back. So Sam said you have quite a busi-ness opportunity on your hands?"

"She did?"

Greg looked at Sam, "This is the guy, right?"

Sam looked at Owen and shrugged, "Owen, you already know my boyfriend, Greg."

Owen nearly fell back into his chair. Sam was dating Greg Masters! He'd just begun to wrap his head around Sam and Greg, Greg and Sam, when Lisa got up from the table to introduce herself to Greg.

"Greg, really nice to meet you. Would you and Sam care to join us for dinner?"

It all happened so fast, Owen could hardly understand what was going on and why the wait staff was now pulling up extra chairs to their table. But the situation quickly got comfortable.

Over appetizers, Owen learned the story of how Greg and Sam had gotten together. After talking to Owen on the phone and understanding the situation with Lisa, Sam decided to get off her flight and head back to the Rio. She was able to get Lisa to go meet with her in person and explained the whole situation.

And who did Sam meet at the bar, right after that meeting? Greg Masters, of course. And why wouldn't they hit it off? They were both smart and driven. They quickly shared the story of their four-month courtship. Things seemed to be going really well.

Over a delicious family-style course of pastas, it was Owen's turn to update the status of ReBicycle. Owen had every intention of keeping in touch with Sam over the break, but he had always been bad about staying in contact with long-distance friends.

As soon as he'd gotten back from Vegas, Owen let everyone at ReBicycle go. It was hard to do, but he had no other options. He had hired all those people way too soon, based on a very shaky business model and a lot of hype and vanity metrics. He had tried to scale a bad idea for a product people didn't actually want, and he had dragged them along for the ride by treating an idea—a startup—as if it were a smaller version of a big company. Now, Owen was literally starting from scratch, and he knew it would create unnecessary pressure and expense to keep his employees on the payroll with nothing to do while he searched for a work-able business model. He wanted to make sure he wasn't rushing into anything again. Surprisingly, the employees all seemed to take it pretty well. They responded from a place of understanding, and many were eager for him to find what he was looking for so that they could come back. Looking back, Owen realized that he hadn't done as good a job shielding them from the stark realities of ReBicycle 1.0 as he'd thought, so they just weren't as shocked as he expected.

That left Owen, Lisa, and the college kid he found on Craigslist, who helped him put bikes together. They were literally starting from scratch.

He had figured out in Vegas that bike shares had a real migraine problem in purchasing bicycle fleets; now he had to make sure that they would buy his solution. If he could crack this puzzle and find a problem/solution fit, each bike share could be responsible for consistent orders for hundreds of bikes per year.

Owen created an initial prototype, a bike he called the "Street Smart." It was a fixed-gear bike, so it was much lighter and easier to maintain but also had a three-hub option that allowed it to have the oomph on hills that single-gear bikes traditionally lacked. More importantly, it was made completely out of the most popular and easy-to-find parts that ReBicycle could procure. The cost to build five of them and add a nice little paint job was only 1,500 bucks. Owen spent another $500 on shipping to have them done up nice and delivered to city planning offices in four different cities and one directly to Shawn Malloy.

One month later, the verdict was in—ReBicycle was a success! Yes, a success at getting people to say they liked the bikes but not actually ordering any. However, Santa Fe's councilman had sent Owen a sketch. It was a god-awful sketch of a bike, but from the writing around the picture and based on where the arrows pointed, Owen was able to figure out what the guy wanted. Bigger handlebars. Thicker tires to deal with sandy and brick roads. A horn possibly? In other words, a bicycle built specifically for the roads and climate of Santa Fe.

Shawn Malloy was even more blunt, "The great people of Charlotte want a bicycle to match them. They want to ride the Charlotte Racer or the Charlotte Cycle. In Charlotte, we pride ourselves on sometimes not being street smart but polite and savvy. I don't know if I want to ride the Street Smart. That's a little too New York sounding for me."

Assumption not validated. A one-size-fits-all-cities bike would not work. It was right after shipping these and getting the first feedback that he and Lisa had figured out a more efficient way to move forward.

"So wait. You're going to send another bicycle to Shawn Malloy?" Lisa asked.

"Of course. He gave me what he wanted, and I can build it in about a week."

"I'm sure you can build it. But why? Why not do a digital design and send that?" Lisa had quickly understood the concept of spending the least amount of time and money to test their various assumptions.

"Because . . . well . . . bikes need to be appreciated in person."

"Owen! It costs you what?—30 bucks in time and work to make a good to scale sketch? That's one-tenth of what the bike costs and after shipping and whatever else, you're just spending unnecessary money. Shawn Malloy isn't shipping these bikes back to you, right?"

"I wouldn't expect him to. But we're at the final table of the World Series, babe. I've now got the funds to ship these bik—"

"Whoa. Hold on." Lisa had quickly become an invaluable partner in their venture. "That's how we got in this mess in the first place. If finding customers and testing your assumptions is the right way to launch a new business, then it shouldn't matter whether we have more money to spend or not. We shouldn't just be flushing it down the toilet because we can. We can't be pushing physical bikes to every 500-person town in America just so they can test the product. Not until we prove that people will pay money for these. Everything else is just a marketing tactic."

"So what? Demand the bikes back?"

"No! Hold their feet to the fire. Send them high-quality designs and then call and call some more and demand something. Didn't you say that we need them to commit to giving us something of value? Otherwise, we'll never know if they think our product is truly a solution for their problem."

"We're not in a position to demand anything, honey."

"Like hell we aren't! We're solving a migraine problem! They need us! If they want to see a physical bike, you've got to ask for something in return. Like you are willing to ship one test bike if they preorder at least 10 bikes. And then we build in the caveats, like they're allowed to make only so many changes to the final product, and they can get a refund if the bikes are not up to the quality specified, or something like that."

"We could do that." Owen could hardly believe how much Lisa had learned and how much she was helping.

"That's the small bet we need to be making, O. These sketches are the shortest path to our customer or to get them to their ultimate action or whatever Sam called it."

And their strategy worked. Owen had indeed sent out high-quality sketches to Shawn Malloy and others, along with a letter explaining that if they wanted more products, they had to place an order. Shawn Malloy and his boss had ended up requiring what must have been nearly 100 e-mails back and forth, but they'd finally ordered 30 test bikes.

Owen had to admit that the 100 or so e-mails might have been time consuming, but they were a lot cheaper than sending more bikes. Athens, Georgia, and Temple, Texas, had been easier to deal with, but both had ordered only 10 test bikes. St. Paul, Minnesota, had been the big catch. They'd put down an option for 100 bikes pending confirmation by the city council. Two months later, though, ReBicycle was still waiting on the city council.

That left Ann Arbor. Owen's contact there, Jim, had initially declined Owen's e-mail, but lo and behold, he'd recently begun e-mailing ReBicycle again, and now his questions were getting very specific. Yeah, you're not supposed to count your chickens before they hatch, but Jim in Ann Arbor was up to something, and hopefully it involved a big order. After all, Lansing, Michigan, had just bought 20 test bikes.

And that was the beauty of the digital sketches. They had allowed ReBicycle to quickly expand beyond the set number of cities they had initially targeted, because they weren't sending out physical bikes. Now, Owen had an Excel sheet with promising cities listed in sets of five. Five was a good target group.

By the second month, there was a pattern—send out targeted messages to five cities with new wording, new designs, new whatever the assumption was. Wait two days. Follow up with a phone call. Wait another day to really test interest and then finally make them the offer about shipping the bike if they preorder. The success rate was nearly 50 percent and getting higher. In the big picture, what it meant was that ReBicycle had just celebrated making its 150th bike share bike. Not a huge number, but it was significantly more progress in four months than Owen had made over the previous year.

He had learned that even when you find a migraine problem, crafting a solution requires constant vigilance and readjustment.

In fact, this scientific approach was working so well at growing initial customer demand that Owen started testing his assumptions about other parts of the business. To validate his assumptions about his supply of bike parts, he contacted potential suppliers and found out that they definitely did not always have a constant source of extra parts. He also found out that their supply fluctuated depending on the season. Because his previous volume had been so low, Owen had never had to worry about having enough bike parts, but trying to fill an order of 2,000 bikes for a single bike share could create a whole new set of problems if he wasn't smart about promises on fulfillment and delivery times.

And that was just one assumption about his supply chain. Owen also tested assumptions about his manufacturing process by learning just how tightly he could store the bicycles without damaging them, and how many employees he'd need per how many bikes (i.e., should he account for one employee for every 50 bikes sold? 100 bikes sold?).

That's right—ReBicycle was hiring again! Slowly, but now Owen had rehired three of his employees full time to help him assemble the bikes, work on designs, and take phone calls about repairs and maintenance. It was important work, but frankly, it had begun eating up way, way too much of Owen's time and it wasn't really helping him grow the business. After all, you don't validate an assumption about oiling a fixed gear—you teach somebody how to do it and they teach other people how to do it.

Owen was finally confident in the business model he was creating. It wasn't all guesses anymore. He had gotten really good at using little bets to test his assumptions and not spend a lot of time or money going too far in the wrong direction. He had finally figured out how to play the hand that he was dealt.

Both Sam and Greg seemed really impressed as Owen told the story of ReBicycle 2.0. Sam couldn't stop asking questions about what they were testing and how, but she seemed satisfied and almost proud at every response Owen and Lisa were giving her.

Over dessert, they were finally able to turn the spotlight on Sam.

"And what about you, Sam? What are you doing?" Owen had asked.

"I'm staying busy . . . I've started to give a new talk at conferences that's been really well received."

"Yeah . . . what about?"

"My talk is about this guy who has a bike business and literally goes about it in the worst way possible until he has a terrible wreck and an epiphany that he needs to start from scratch."

"Ha . . . you're yanking my chain."

"Serious as a heart attack, Owen. Based on a true story, too."

The table exploded in laughter. Owen had been right. This was going to be a very different dinner than his last experience at Il Greco.

Chapter 43

Don't Commit All-In until You Prove That Customers Want Your Product and There's a Business Model to Support It

O wen woke up refreshed. He hadn't remembered Il Greco being that good. It was definitely one of the best nights that he and Lisa had shared in a long time.

He was enjoying a morning cup of coffee and catching up on the paper while Lisa slept. Pregnancy was forcing her to get some extra rest these days.

Owen heard a knock on the door and made his way to see who it was. He had only opened it a crack before Pitchford thrust the door open and strolled into the room.

"Good morning, sunshine!"

"Good morning to you, too, Pitchford."

"I wasn't talking to you, O."

Lisa was still waking up and it took her a second to realize Pitchford was staring at her. "Pitchford!"

"Hey, Owen told me 9 A.M. for breakfast and it was hell trying to get a reservation."

"Can you give me like 10 minutes and perhaps a smidgen of privacy to get ready?" Lisa negotiated.

"They're going to give our table away. They told me as much when I got the reservation."

"Okay, okay." Owen was already dressed; he didn't need much getting ready for breakfast. He grabbed his Buckeyes baseball hat and a letter he had left by the front door. "Come on, Pitchford. Let's go down and get the table. Babe, we'll see you in a couple minutes."

"Thank you!" She was clearly relieved. Owen liked to come to her rescue, especially if it meant he got to eat sooner.

"Lisa, free mimosas only for another 30 minutes!"

"See if you can get me a pitcher, Pitch!" She joked back as they walked out of the room.

As they walked down the hall to the elevators, Owen told Pitchford he had to make a quick stop by the front desk to mail something.

"Forget to pay some bills?"

Owen smiled, "Not quite."

"What is it?"

"It's kind of a long explanation."

"Owen, what's in the letter?"

"Well, Lisa and I ran into Sam at dinner last night . . ."

"Oh my God, is this a confessional letter you're sending to Lisa? Wait, that doesn't make any sense. Is this a break-up letter, like what happened last night can never happen again between us, kind of letter?"

"Easy, Pitch. Sam and her boyfriend ended up having dinner with me and Lisa, and we spent a lot of time talking about ReBicycle."

"Okay, okay, get to the sexy part of the story. The confessional."

"The sexy part is that over dessert Sam offered to make a pretty sizeable investment in ReBicycle."

"Whoa. That is a lot less interesting than I was hoping for, but still really cool. Congrats, man! How much she going to give you?"

"Well, I'm not sure. But this letter is me declining her offer."

"That's crazy. Can I read it?"

"Well, I already sealed it. And it's kind of . . ." Pitchford grabbed the letter out of Owen's hand and held it up like he was going to open it.

"We'll get another envelope from the front desk. May I?"

"Go ahead."

Pitchford opened the letter and began to read it out loud.

Dear Sam,

I really appreciate your interest in potentially investing in ReBicycle. I'm putting together this letter in response to your inquiry for additional information.

The past year has been full of unexpected setbacks and yet I honestly cannot say I've ever been more optimistic for the growth and expansion of the company. We've gone from attempting to create an online platform for bicycle consumers to developing an invaluable product for government and quasi-government bike share programs around the country. Indeed, as I write this, I've just received an e-mail inquiry from a city in the Netherlands asking about our bicycles. Our new focus has not only taken us across the United States, but is now developing into the opportunity to grow internationally.

ReBicycle has finally found a migraine problem worth solving and new customers have started finding us without any prompting. This is something that seemed like a pipe dream just four months ago and it's slowly becoming our reality.

With that said, and although I am extremely humbled and grateful for your interest in investing in ReBicycle, I think it might be too soon to begin investment discussions. Yes, we've identified a real migraine problem. Yes, we've been able to prove that customers want our product through some initial sales. But we have yet to complete a full transaction where ReBicycle will supply an entire fleet for a specific bike share program or figure out what levels of maintenance and support will be required. There are simply too many assumptions still left unresolved in this business model, and the last thing I want to do is prematurely scale a new concept. It would just be too risky to put a lot of money toward executing on an idea before it's ready, and I'm not ready to go all-in quite yet.

But I'd really like to revisit this conversation in about six months when we've hopefully had time to test and prove the remainder of those assumptions that pose the greatest amount of risk to our current business model. Plus, I think it might increase the value of the company and necessitate a larger investment :-). So I appreciate your patience and your continued mentorship. I can't thank you enough for the impact you've made both on the company and me personally.

On a personal note, I didn't get a chance to tell you at dinner that Lisa and I just found out that we're having a boy. Looking forward to introducing you to future ReBicycle employee and Tour de France winner, Samuel Chase.

—Owen

Chapter 44

The Strength of Your Initial Idea, or Starting Hand, Is Always Relative

"Ladies and gentlemen, welcome to the, uh, final table of the World Series of Po—"

"Cut. Can we do that again? You had an 'uh' in there."

"Got it. Ladies and gentlemen, welcome to the final table of the World Series of Poker!"

"Perfect."

Overhearing that exchange as soon as he arrived on the tournament floor, Owen knew who was running the show. It may have been his 10 grand that got him here (okay, Pitchford's 10 grand), but it was ESPN's baby now. They would be broadcasting the final table live, which meant that producers and announcers and lots of other

269

staff were trying to make sure everything sounded and looked good because there was no postproduction. The nine players themselves might as well have been afterthoughts.

Owen was definitely feeling anxious, or nervous. Whatever it was, it was making his stomach rumble. By the time all of the players were announced by name and then all of the sponsors were announced by name and all of the "distinguished guests" were announced by name, Owen felt like he had spent a solid hour of just sitting at the table, grinning like a schmuck at Lisa, Pitchford, and the audience and waiting for play to start. Finally, though, the floor emcee said the magic words, "Dealer, shuffle up and deal!"

The players had drawn ping-pong balls with numbers on them to determine seating, and Owen had drawn number 2. That meant being in an early spot away from the blinds which were now ridiculous and it meant an easy fold on the first hand when he got a 10-something. Something part visceral and part physical happened as he folded. It was like his mind said, "Oh yeah, I remember doing this," and all the nervousness seemed to go away. Just like that. It was just another poker table.

After a complete round went by, it was obvious the one-hour gentlemen's agreement was in effect. Everybody was either afraid to make the first move or didn't want to risk anything this early.

Several hands in, Owen was finally happy with his starting pair. He looked around the table to see the other players' reactions to their cards. This might be the final table of the World Series of Poker, but these players were still human; there was still intelligence here to gather. Someone at the table made a bet and Greg Masters, in a later position, raised. There was a sizeable bet waiting for Owen by the time the action got to him. He looked down at his cards again to confirm what he previously saw, a pocket pair of aces.

This was going to be fun.

Players to meet:
- Phil Helmuth
- Annie Duke
- Tony Hsieh
- Nathan Sanko
- Phil Ivy
-

Adam Walker
703-001-4332
- wants to test
drive my wrangler
July 27

Rio spa conf. - 1:30pm
- ask for Laura Marcusse

- met Kyle Juvers - public something in Chicago
       - interested in getting involved in
          Goodwill Board
- met Owen Chase - ReBicycle
    What is his deal?
       ↳ Loves his idea more than ~~reality~~
          more than his customers
    Can I help?
       → Does he even want help?
          or is he just going for luck?

Questions for Owen

who is the customer?
what is their migraine problem?

① Do <u>people</u> <u>want</u> <u>it</u>? ⟶ what is the shortest
path to the ultimate
customer action?

② Is there a business model to
support it?

Owen's Customers
- who are they?
  ↳ where do we find groups/lists of them?
- what is their problem?
- is it a migraine?
- what are they currently doing to fix it?
- on a scale of 1-10, how much does
  it impact their lives?
- what are their bigger problems?
- how much money would they spend
  to fix their prob?

Day 2 Play !!!
Table 115, seat 6

273

★ IDEA - Handsocks   July 9

   Customer: women w/
     office jobs
   Problem: they are
   cold indoors,
    but don't want to wear a sweater everyday
   Ultimate Customer Action: Get women to
     order handsocks online
   Who to interview: Go to Virginia's office
   & talk to women there.
    - Also, Sprint, Polsinelli, + Groupon offices

   Test landing page to see what %
 of visitors click the pay button
 or are interested in a discount on the fix
    + enter their cc info

ReBicycle
   - hasn't found a migraine problem to solve
What should Owen do?
     ↳ Create luck! - how?
① Do not operate on tilt! A fear
    of failure is not a strategy.

Luck (cont.)

② Make small bets Owen can afford to lose to find the opportunities → continue to interview potential customers to find the migraines.

③ Reduce the risk of failure by figuring out which business plan assumptions are ☒right or wrong.

④ Reduce the risk of failure by finding a real problem worth solving.

⑤ Once Owen finds an opportunity, reduce the risk of failure by simulating the ultimate customer action before he invests much time or money.

Bottom line

Owen can create luck by getting customers as soon as possible & not wasting time or money building something no one needs or wants.

Clubs!!!
What happened.?!?
How did I miss that FLUSH

Bubble girl Sam

Bike shares for Owen - Is he ready to go
All-In?

Owen's |All In Challenge|

① Is he mentally prepared to run a startup?
  · Has he overcome operating on tilt
    his fear of failure?
  · Does he know how to identify
    opportunities through small bets
    he can afford to lose?

② Has he identified a problem worth solving?
  · Is it a migraine level pain?
  · Did his specific customer segment
    articulate the pain + beg for the solution?

All In Challenge (cont.)

③ Has he confirmed that customers <u>will buy</u> his product to solve their problem?
- What is the shortest path to the ultimate customer action?

④ Is there a business model to support this company?
- Is it capable of making the kind of revenue Owen is looking for?
- Does he have access to the people, capital, and skills necessary to execute the plan?

WANT MORE?!

Go to:

www. _AllInStartup.com_ to:

- Take the All In Challenge

- Download the full list of
  Rules for Customer Interviews

- Find a book club discussion guide

- Get suggested curriculum for using
  All In Startup in a classroom

- And More!

Acknowledgments

Regrettably, one important point I was unable to cover in this book is that it's extremely difficult to launch anything on your own. It usually takes the hard work of a lot of talented team members to make anything of substance happen. I tried to refer to several members of Owen's team throughout the book, but for the sake of brevity, I minimized their interactions.

I've been very lucky to work with so many incredible people in various ventures throughout the years, and this project is no different. So I want to take this opportunity to acknowledge the hard work and contributions of so many generous individuals who helped make *All In Startup* a reality.

I want to thank my husband, Jason, who read every single draft and patiently discussed each plot change. It's not easy to read 200-page drafts over and over again. But Jason attacked each one with a fresh sense of enthusiasm. I'm lucky to have his support and counsel.

I want to thank Reverse Book Club (RBC) and its members Adam Walker, Nathan and Laura Sanko, and Kyle Juvers. I knew that one of the hardest parts of writing a book would be holding myself accountable and having the discipline to make revisions and keep moving forward. I assembled four of my favorite people, who had a varied set of skills, to meet every two weeks and help me complete the story. Our RBC meetings were some of the most fun get-togethers I've ever attended. We went out and played poker together, talked over each chapter and the plot week by week, and came up with a set of interesting characters that made the business concepts memorable.

Adam is a cyclist with a fantastic sense of humor who helped add some levity to the story. Nathan is an entrepreneur and angel investor who has a lot of experience in poker tournament play. Laura is an entrepreneur in her own right, in addition to being a professional mixed martial arts fighter. She was the inspiration for all of Sam's virtues and none of her vices. Kyle also brought a lot of poker knowledge to the story, and his legendary attention to detail was absolutely necessary to keep our gregarious RBC meetings organized and on task.

Once the plot was set and it was time to get to the business of writing, I turned to my good friend Owen Morris for help. As an editor, Owen taught me how to baste the business principles I was trying to convey with a juicy coat of fiction. He helped me give edge and depth to the individual characters, and it is out of gratitude for his mentorship and his time that I named Owen Chase after him.

Because I'm a believer in the idea of understanding your customers and creating a product that solves their problems, I had a number of entrepreneurs read the various drafts to see if the message resonated with what they were going through. I rewrote the manuscript seven times. The following individuals read through the various drafts and gave me substantive feedback that made the final product what it is: Joanne Brownstein Jarvi, Nathan Kurtz, Adam Berk, Jon Kohrs, Aaron Beaty, Sam and Julie Meers, Maria Flynn, Shashi Jain, Philip Broughton, Ted Zollar, Tom Boozer, Timothy Bovard, Brent Beshore, Bob Dorf, Harry Campbell, Derek Andersen, Tony Hsieh, and Nick Seguin.

It doesn't matter how good your work product is if no one ever reads it. Jo-Lynne Worley and Joanie Shoemaker instantly saw the potential for what this book could become and tenaciously represented me to make sure that it made it to the bookshelves. I'm eternally grateful for their hard work and expert guidance through the publishing process.

I also want to thank Laura Gachko at Wiley for taking a chance on what is admittedly a very unconventional approach to a business book. A big thank you to Judy Howarth, Tula Batanchiev, Stacey Fischkelta, and all of the other professionals at Wiley for working so hard to make the final version of *All In Startup* something we are all very proud of.

I'm grateful to several close friends for helping me tell the story behind *All In Startup* so that the book could be on the radar screen of entrepreneurship educators: Amanda Schnieders, Ryan Baird, Owen Morris, Nodir "Bek" Abdullayev, Joe Stokely, Ben Edwards, and Taylor Brown.

I want to thank Steve Blank for opening my eyes to the world of evidence-based entrepreneurship and for his tireless dedication to helping entrepreneurs build successful enterprises. The world would be a better place if more people heard his message.

Thank you to Thom Ruhe and the team at the Kauffman Foundation for giving me the chance to help advance Mr. K's vision through my work as a senior fellow. I'm lucky to work with such a great team pursuing such an important mission.

A big thanks to Dean Pitchford for turning me on to fiction and its power to communicate ideas.

Finally, I want to thank my son, True. As I write this, you are only four months old, but you are already totally awesome. Thanks for all the smiles.

About the Author

A refugee of the Soviet Union, Diana Kander entered America as an eight-year-old resident of subsidized housing in Brooklyn, New York. By the time she was an American citizen, she had perfected her skills as a capitalist, selling flea market goods to grade-school classmates at a markup.

Today, Diana is a successful entrepreneur, having founded and sold a number of ventures, and a senior fellow at the Ewing Marion Kauffman Foundation, the largest nonprofit in the world dedicated to entrepreneurship and education. A Georgetown-educated attorney who left a successful practice to launch her first company, Diana draws on her experience as a founder, investor, and academic to design and implement curriculum in educational institutions and the private sector.

A sought-out public speaker, consultant, and writer, Diana has advised startup founders and Fortune 500 executives on her methodology for launching customer-focused products and services and developing an entrepreneurial mindset throughout an organization.

Diana lives in Columbia, Missouri, with her high school sweetheart/best friend/husband, Jason, and their awesome son, True.

■ ■ ■

Find out more at www.DianaKander.com